ANIMAL SPIRITS

LIVING WISDOM

ANIMAL SPIRITS

NICHOLAS J. SAUNDERS

SERIES CONSULTANT: **PIERS VITEBSKY**

MACMILLAN

IN ASSOCIATION WITH
DUNCAN BAIRD PUBLISHERS

Animal Spirits

First published in Great Britain in 1995

A DBP book
published by
Macmillan Reference Books
a division of Macmillan
Publishers Limited
Cavaye Place
London SW10 9PG
and Basingstoke

A CIP catalogue record for this book is available from the British Library

ISBN 0-333-63846-8

Conceived, created and designed by
Duncan Baird Publishers
Sixth Floor
Castle House
75-76 Wells Street
London W1P 3RE

10 9 8 7 6 5 4 3 2 1

Associate author: Clifford Bishop

Editor: Penelope Miller

Consultant: Tuppence Stone
Consultant editors: Peter Bently, Jack Tresidder

Designer: Steve Painter
Picture research: Nadine Bazar

Typeset in Times NR MT
Colour reproduction by
Colourscan, Singapore
Printed in Singapore

Contents

Introduction

When Marco Polo returned to Venice in 1295 and described his Asian experiences – the great zoos, which really existed, with their tigers, rhinos, cheetahs and lynxes – he was branded "Messer Milioni, the man who talks in millions", a boastful liar. Another medieval writer, Jean de Bourgogne, wrote an entirely fabricated account of his own travels which included vegetable lambs, mermaids and serpent-footed Indians, and even included fantasticated gobbets of Marco Polo's own memoirs. It became the most popular travel book in Europe, and remained a standard reference until the 17th century.

There are two interpretations of these events: that observable, unadorned nature is more incredible than anything man can invent; or that, building on the foundations of nature, humans have developed a kind of parallel, fabulous animal kingdom which is more emotionally and aesthetically satisfying to us than the real world. In a way, both interpretations would be equally correct.

Just as, for many years, we needed the horse to carry us into battle, so we needed the idea of the horse to reassure us that our soul's passage to the spirit world would be swift and certain. And in the imagination, creatures that were beyond our control – or understanding – could be "domesticated", and made use of. The real animals might be obscured, or lost altogether, within the paraphernalia of ritual and human need. But they are always to be found somewhere in the jumble of ideas that surround them. This book follows the tracks of living animals through the human imagination.

"Building Noah's Ark", from the 1423 Bedford Book of Hours. In the Book of Genesis, God told Noah: "And of every living thing of all flesh, two of every sort shalt thou bring into the ark."

The Shared World

The apelike ancestors of humankind had very little involvement with other animals. Apart from the occasional egg, insect or carrion, they ate mostly fruit, leaves and shoots. Because they were nomadic within their particular territory, and therefore left no permanent domestic detritus, they did not even share their lives with fleas.

As the forests dwindled some 50 million years ago, our ancestors took to the plains. There they had to learn to hunt, and their study of, and fascination with, other animals began. Much more recently, early humans painted pictures of their prey on rocks and cave walls. The paintings reflect the awe in which they held these creatures, and humanity's relationship with animals has always reflected this ambivalence: we admire, and are fascinated most by, that which we fear or wish to kill. We have created exotic new breeds, yet we have exterminated entire species. We have cosseted pets, yet treated farm animals as factory-produced units. We have turned animals into gods, yet forced them to perform demeaning tricks to confirm us in our superiority.

A fresco, dating from 2130BC, which shows an Egyptian nobleman, with his wife and his daughter, using a cat to flush a variety of waterfowl from cover.

Animals and ourselves

Among the earliest evidence of humankind's relationship with animals are the paintings made on cave walls by Cro-Magnon man more than 20,000 years ago. The animals depicted are invariably strong, or dangerous, or swift. It has been suggested that the paintings are a form of sympathetic magic, an attempt to control the beast through its representation. However, close scrutiny of these most ancient of cave paintings shows that the hooves depicted are not bearing any weight. The animals seem dead, and stretched out on their sides. The cave paintings reveal man's primordial relationship with other animals: they are trophies of the hunt.

More than 10,000 years ago in the Fertile Crescent of the Middle East, humans began to cultivate the grasses that would eventually become wheat. Animal bones discovered at their settlements reveal that these people were still hunting for all their meat. The domestication of animals began about 1,000 years later, with goats and sheep, probably when the early farmers realized that these pests, which had been attracted by their crops, could be more profitably captured than killed. In this way they provided not just occasional meat and hides, but also regular milk, wool and labour.

The more exotic and dangerous animals, meanwhile, were assuming the status of totems. They were adopted as the spiritually significant emblems of a people and, as tribes merged or were conquered, evolved into an animal pantheon. Even here, human relationships with animals were often utilitarian. In ancient Egypt it was a capital offence to kill a cat or an ibis, but thousands of these animals were involved in burial

PEOPLE AND PETS

People may have kept pets even before they began to herd animals for food. Fossil records show that the dog was already domesticated by 9600BC. The first pets were probably baby animals brought back from the hunt, and initially intended for the pot. Some of these would be adopted by the hunter's children, and eventually develop into valued companions. The early Native Americans kept wolves, bears and bison as pets. Increasing urbanization does not seem to deter people from having pets, but it is altering the species chosen. In the United States the number of pet dogs rose from 48 million to 51 million in the 1980s. The number of cats, which are better adapted to cities, rose from 35 million to 56 million in the same period.

In Papua New Guinea, pigs are treasured possessions. Women may suckle piglets brought back from the hunt, and mourn for them when they are finally slaughtered.

Fashionable European women of the 19th century were obsessed with feather accessories, and one London feather dealer in the 1850s bought 32,000 hummingbirds in a single purchase. In many South American cultures, the tiny, jewel-like hummingbird was associated with bloodletting and sacrifice, but even here had a decorative function. Aztec bone bloodletters often had a hummingbird supping from a flower carved into the blunt end. Among the Olmec people, perforating tools were frequently carved from jadeite in the shape of a hummingbird.

ceremonies, and an examination of their mummified remains shows that they were mostly young specimens, who had died of a broken neck. It seems that, unknown to the worshipping public, the priests set up a factory farming system for sacred beasts.

As humans and animals evolved closer together, people developed a respect for more than just a creature's speed, strength or rarity, or its perceived courage. It became clear that many animals possessed mysterious powers. Bees were valued as weather forecasters, returning to the hive and becoming agitated before a storm. Modern experiments show that they behave similarly in the presence of an electrical field, and it is likely that they sense the electromagnetic charges that build up in storm clouds. Migrating birds are also skilled weather forecasters, capable of detecting the minute drops in air pressure that anticipate good conditions for flight. This skill is probably a by-product of the in-built barometer that allows birds to judge and maintain their altitude. Birds are also acutely sensitive to any

Camels are essential for the survival of nomadic peoples such as the Tuareg and the Bedouin. A camel can sense water from 25 miles (40km) away, and in between drinks it can lose 40 per cent of its body water without suffering. In the absence of food it survives on fat stored in its hump. The camel is not only a beast of burden for the nomads: it provides meat, milk, wool and dung for fuel.

ANIMALS ON DISPLAY

The earliest record of a menagerie is on an Egyptian tomb wall built more than 4,000 years ago. Animals have been collected and displayed as symbols of wealth and power ever since. The Aztec Emperor Montezuma even kept deformed and albino humans among an animal collection so large that it required 600 keepers and the slaughter of 500 turkeys a day just to feed the big cats. Until this century, even humanely kept animals used to be locked in scrubbed, cell-like cages, and became bored and unhealthy, but modern zoos are as much concerned with conservation and education as with entertainment.

The safari park is a modern variant on the zoo which allows the animals to wander free – within limits – and keeps the visiting humans locked up in their cars.

low-frequency rumbling, which could explain the instances of their singing loudly at night just before earthquakes.

Some animal skills and senses were specially exaggerated by selective breeding. All domestic dogs are the same species, and can interbreed. Their common ancestor is the wolf, and they still show an ancestral tendency to cooperate, to hunt in packs, and to depend on a group leader – a role most often filled by humans. By emphasizing traits found naturally in the wolf, humans have produced a huge variety of specialized breeds, such as retrievers (which exaggerate the wolf's habit of sharing its food with the other pack members), dalmatians (coach dogs which emulate the wolf's habit of tracking its prey over long distances) and pointers (which freeze on spotting prey, to indicate its position to the pack).

Although humans have developed many such fruitful alliances with former pests and enemies, our relationship with most of the animal kingdom is one of hostility. Animal pests still consume some 20 per cent of India's total food production. More directly, humans are host to numerous internal parasites, such as tapeworms, which live in the intestine and can grow up to 40 feet (13 metres) long, as well as the external bloodsuckers such as mosquitoes, fleas and bedbugs. The 175 species of *Anopheles* mosquitoes also transmit another dangerous animal – the single-celled *Plasmodium*, which causes malaria (one of the most ancient known diseases, first described by Hippocrates in the 5th century BC). Mosquitoes also transmit nematode worms, which are possibly the most widespread animals on earth, and can cause the painful swelling of elephantiasis.

Parrots were prized by the Aztecs for their feathers as much as for their gifts of mimicry, which vary from species to species. No one knows why parrots imitate human speech. In the wild, they are only reluctant mimics of other birds and animals. In medieval China, parrots were supposed to inform on adulterous wives.

Evolution and breeding

Charles Darwin did not invent the theory of evolution. In 1809, the year of Darwin's birth, the French naturalist Lamarck suggested that the stresses an environment places on an animal cause it to develop some useful feature, which it then passes on to its offspring, who develop it further. Over the course of generations this useful feature – for example, the long neck of the giraffe – becomes progressively more exaggerated. Darwin's contribution to evolution theory was the idea of natural selection, which is now broadly accepted. According to Darwin, the giraffe's long neck arose because some of its ancestors were accidentally born with longer than average necks. They were better able to reach leaves high up in the trees, and as a result were more likely to survive, breed and pass on their characteristics. Evolution does

Fossils of extinct creatures such as the trilobite are most likely to be found in sedimentary rocks such as limestone. They can be dated by measuring their levels of natural radioactivity, which declines with age.

not progress by design, but by a number of accidents, most of which nature obliterates, while "selecting" a few for survival. A form of natural selection probably even predated life, acting on the large, self-replicating molecules that floated in the primeval soup some 3,000 million years ago. Collections of these complex molecules began to form membranes made of proteins and fats about 2,000 million years ago, and in the process created the first, single-celled, living things. The first multi-celled life appeared nearly 1,000 million years later.

The family trees of modern animals can be traced by their shared structural features. The amphibians, reptiles, birds and mammals all have pentadactyl (five-toed) limbs, which have been variously modified for walking, climbing, swimming or flying. In some cases toes

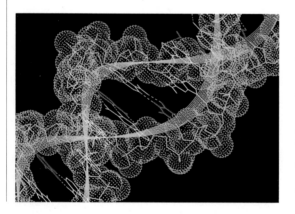

The double-helix spiral of DNA contains a "code" that tells cell structures what proteins to make, and as such is essentially a blueprint for building bodies. A gene is a stretch of DNA that is some thousands of "code-words" long. Sexual reproduction passes on half of each parent's genes to the offspring, adding up to a complete set. Humans share more than 98 per cent of their genetic structure with pygmy chimpanzees, indicating a common ancestry.

have atrophied. The wing of the bird has only three fused digits, and the horse has just one toe on each foot. Yet both these adaptations have developed from the pentadactyl limb, which itself can be traced back to bones in the fins of fossil fishes, from which the first amphibians evolved.

When humans started domesticating animals they found that desirable characteristics could be preserved and exaggerated by selective breeding. Sheep and goats were bred to provide more wool, meat and fat. Behaviour could also be modified, and cattle were at first bred mainly for docility, and only later for better milk and meat production. (Their ancestor, the ferocious aurochs, died out as recently as 1627, in Poland.) Animals that have some kind of herd structure, such as cattle, horses and especially dogs, seem to have been the easiest to breed into many different forms and temperaments. Solitary animals, such as cats and ferrets, although among the earliest species to be domesticated, are still remarkably similar to their wild forms. Some herd animals, such as yaks and camels, are also relatively unaltered by humans, because their value lies in their natural adaptation to a harsh environment.

Convergent evolution occurs when widely separated animals face similar environmental stresses, and evolve similar solutions. The South American plains, the African savanna and the Australian bush have all produced large, flightless birds, capable of running swiftly for long distances to evade predators. The rhea, ostrich and emu are "ecological analogues" of each other: they occupy the same niche in their respective ecosystems.

HORSE AND RIDER

The ancestor of the horse was the terrier-sized, forest-browser *Eohippus*, which died out some 50 million years ago. The modern horse, which appeared 2 million years ago, evolved as the forests dwindled and grasslands spread, creating the need for a longer-legged animal capable of rapid flight. Wild asses were domesticated in the Nile Valley and Sumeria between 3000BC and 2000BC.

At about the same time the Eurasian wild horse, the ancestor of all domestic horses, was tamed by the steppe-nomads. The large, powerfully built farm horses common throughout Europe, such as the shire horse, were originally bred to carry knights in heavy armour into battle. The less armoured Arabs favoured more slender, faster breeds.

Przewalski's horse, which once covered the eastern steppes, is the only surviving Eurasian wild horse. There are probably fewer than a hundred left.

Looking within

Darwin's assertion that human origins were unquestionably animal profoundly undermined the traditional European view that whereas humans might sometimes act in what was seen as a "bestial" – that is, irrational or violent – manner, any resemblance to animal behaviour was coincidental and not intrinsic to the higher nature with which God had endowed the greatest of His creatures. After Darwin, philosophers and psychologists explored the idea that "animal" human behaviour was not aberrant but innate and instinctual. Friedrich Nietzsche (1844-1900) argued that people should acknowledge only their primitive will and instincts, the elemental animal drive for life free from cultural constraint. Society and religion, he said, along with their constraints, should be regarded as illusions.

Sigmund Freud (1856–1939) also recognized the irrational forces that drove people, but advocated psychoanalysis to control them. He called humanity's

The Nightmare *by Henry Fuseli (1741–1825). Jung said that images representing the Shadow may appear in dreams, when the ego is dormant and, as Plato put it, "the wild beast in us ... becomes rampant".*

base, primitive, instinct the "id" and its culturally assembled conscience the "superego". The eternal inner struggle

---

ANIMAL KINSHIPS

The concept of a hidden and sinister "animal" side to human nature is alien to Native American traditions, which regard people and animals as possessing the same spiritual essence. It is said that in ancient times they were also physically indistinguishable and that, before their identities became fixed, individuals could metamorphose at will between human and animal forms. Some peoples of the northwest coastal region of North America believe that

their clan ancestors came ashore from the sea and exchanged their animal guises for human ones.

No animals are regarded as closer to people than bears, which sometimes walk on their hind legs and have skeletons seen as resembling those of people, only larger. Many myths depict bears as people who always wear their bear coats in public but remove them in private to reveal their human form. In Navaho belief both bears and humans are represented by the deity known simply as "Two-legged".

Two young Alaskan brown bears adopt what at first glance might appear to be human-like postures to engage in friendly sparring.

between the two often led to disaster, manifested either in the form of personal tragedies such as murder, or collective ones such as war.

According to the later theory of the "collective unconscious" proposed by Carl Gustav Jung (1875–1961), underlying the individual experience of life was an inborn, universal level of psychic experience full of archetypal symbols and images derived from our remotest ancestry. These archetypes included the "Shadow", the "dark side, characterized by inferior, uncivilized or animal qualities". The Shadow's animal dynamism could enhance life if it was honestly confronted and acknowledged. It posed a danger only if the ego, the conscious self, attempted to repress its subconscious urgings.

CALIBAN

In 1611 William Shakespeare put onto the English stage an unusual character who is sometimes seen as inhabiting the borderline between the human and animal worlds. Caliban is described in the list of characters for *The Tempest* as "a savage and deformed slave", and is frequently seen by others in the play as animal or monstrous in appearance. The name Caliban is thought to be in part an anagram of the word cannibal, which is derived from the European version of the name Carib, the native peoples of the Caribbean. The etymology of the name Caliban is indicative of the way in which the European colonists of the 16th and 17th centuries mythologized racial otherness and constructed images of monstrous beings in the new worlds they encountered.

In human culture the snake or serpent has long represented evil and sinister forces. It is often venomous and inhabits dark, subterranean regions, from which it slithers rapidly and silently, without the use of limbs, to attack its victims. In the Bible, a snake led Eve and Adam into a state of sin, and the monster Leviathan was often depicted as a serpent, as in this miniature from a 12th-century English Commentary on the Apocalypse. In the Book of Revelation, the archangel Michael conquers "that old serpent, called the Devil". Yet the serpent may also be perceived as benign: as a dweller in the earth it is associated with the fertility of the soil and the renewal of nature. It symbolized the Aztec earth goddess Coatlicue ("Serpent Skirt").

The animal kingdom

Humans have long been fascinated by the position of animals in the natural order and how to account for their existence, both in relation to humankind and to each other. In the Judaeo-Christian tradition the hierarchy of beasts and the superiority of humans over animals was established by God at the time of the Creation. On the fifth day God created the creatures of sea and air, followed on the sixth day by land animals and, finally, man, his greatest creation, formed "in His own image" to subdue the earth and have dominion "over every living thing" (Genesis i:20–28). Adam named every creature and, according to the bestiaries of medieval Europe, established the first classification of beasts, distinguishing those that were "wild", "useful", "armed" (that is, horned) and "unarmed" (hornless).

The bestiaries made little attempt to order the animal kingdom in a consis-

The first scientific natural histories still tended to class sea mammals as marine counterparts of more familiar terrestrial creatures. The "sea wolf", or elephant seal (top), and sea lion (above) are from the Histoire Naturelle *by de Buffon (1707–88).*

Adam naming the beasts, from a Latin bestiary of 1230 in St John's College, Oxford. After the Bible and other religious texts, bestiaries were the most popular form of illustrated book in medieval Europe. They all derive from a single source known as the Physiologus, *composed in Greek c. AD150, probably in Egypt (the animals described included species such as the ibis). This lost original combined description and myth with Christian moralizing. The European bestiaries shed much of the moralizing content and added some local species to those contained in the* Physiologus.

tent way – they were not even presented in alphabetical order – but there was a tendency to group together domesticated animals, ruminants and the big cats. The classification of animals remained highly unsystematic until the 18th century, when natural history became established as a serious science, prompted in part by the flood of discoveries of animal and plant species by European voyagers and explorers. In 1749 the French naturalist Georges-Louis Leclerc, comte de Buffon, embarked on his monumental *Histoire Naturelle*, the first attempt at a comprehensive, systematic and coherent description of the natural world. At his death in 1788 some 36 volumes of a projected 50 had been published (eight more appeared posthumously).

De Buffon was the first to suggest the existence of long-extinct species. This idea was the starting point for the modern science of paleontology and was the first scientific attempt to account for the existence of fossilized dinosaur

Within years of the discovery of the New World, books such as Reisch's 1508 Pearls of Wisdom *(above) were claiming it as the home of fabulous anthropomorphic creatures.*

bones (traditional explanations included the claim that they were the remains of monsters which had perished in the biblical Flood). De Buffon's proposition that species such as the horse and donkey might be related was an important milestone on the road to the evolutionary theories developed by Lamarck and Darwin in the 19th century.

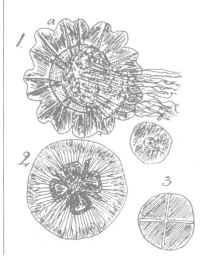

LINNAEUS

The scientific method of classifying living and extinct organisms was developed in its essentials by the Swedish botanist and naturalist Carl von Linné (1707–78), better known by the latinized version of his name, Linnaeus. His system of Latin nomenclature classified every animal and plant according to "genus" and "species" in a way that made clear which animals were related. For example, the genus *Canis* ("Dog") included the species domestic dog (*Canis familiaris*) and common grey wolf (*Canis lupus*). Modern scientists have developed a more elaborate version of the basic Linnean system which classifies by phylum, class, order, family, genus and species.

Linnaeus made these sketches of jellyfish (left), to which he gave the generic name medusae, *on a scientific expedition to Lapland in 1732.*

Rarity and abundance

There are 600 species of bird in Costa Rica, 386 in California and only 200 in Alaska. For mammals, insects and even fish, there is a similar gradient of diversity from the equator to the poles. This is one reason why the destruction of the rainforests is the most serious modern threat to the biological diversity of the planet. The range of species can decline even if the total number of individual animals in a region increases. Since records began, a quarter of all mammal extinctions and a fifth of bird extinctions have been caused by humans introducing alien species to an area. The

In the 1970s, eggs from green turtle nests were artificially incubated and 100,000 hatchlings released into the Caribbean. In the wild, a nest on the low shore is more likely to be disturbed by wave action than a nest higher up, but any hatchlings are more likely to reach the sea. The sex of turtles is determined by the temperature of the nest, which also depends on its position. As nobody knows how many hatchlings from each nest site survive, the sexual composition of the world's green turtle population is unknown; well-meaning but careless conservation may have disturbed its balance.

ENDANGERED SPECIES

The conservation movement has concentrated its attention on large animals that the public finds attractive, even though these are often genetically unsuccessful, and may be bound for extinction even without human interference. The giant panda is descended from carnivorous bears. It would be a carnivore itself if only it were quick or clever enough to catch prey, and there have been reports of pandas worrying sheep. The panda's digestive system is not designed for a vegetable diet, so it must consume tons of bamboo in order to extract very little nourishment. Yet it has no thumb to grip the bamboo, and must use its wristbone. In addition, female pandas are only on heat for a few days in each year, and even then they are often not receptive to males.

The giant panda survives in the wild only in the remote bamboo forests of China.

dodo was largely exterminated by the introduction of pigs to Mauritius. One hitherto undiscovered species of finch is known only from the eleven dead bodies presented to a lighthouse keeper by his cat. But rats, migrating on ships from country to country, have been responsible for more extinctions than any other animal. They are voracious predators, and if unchecked an adult pair can generate a population of nearly half a million in only two years. The black rat, which originated in India, has even been instrumental in decimating human populations, as a carrier of bubonic plague.

Even where alien animals have not wiped out indigenous species, their presence has often been disastrous. The 24 rabbits released in Australia in 1859 soon reached plague proportions – only checked by myxomatosis in 1950 – yet even rabbits have done less damage than cattle, which have reduced 750,000 sq miles (2 million sq km) of land to semi-desert through overgrazing.

Elsewhere, humans have successfully repopulated areas with species on the verge of extinction. By 1962 there were only a handful of oryx antelopes left in the wild. Some were captured and taken to the United States for breeding. Within ten years the last wild oryx were shot, yet from a captive population of 150 the species has been reintroduced to parts of Jordan, Oman and Israel.

For most of their life-cycle, locusts exist as harmless grasshoppers, but periodically they grow wings and migrate in swarms of up to 40,000 *million members, covering 100 sq miles (250 sq km). Such a swarm eats enough in one day to feed 400,000 people for a year.*

Animal intelligence and the soul

The question of whether animals are intelligent, sensate beings entitled to legal and moral rights on the same basis as humans has been seriously debated since the ancient Greeks. However, until the 19th century the view prevailed that animals were inferior in intellect and deserved no special treatment. The medieval Church took Genesis as its guide when it saw animals as created by God to be placed under the command of man. Animals were believed to have souls but were stupid and unreasoning; however, if they harmed humans, they might be consciously evil or possessed and faced execution or excommunication. In 1541 the latter penalty was imposed on a plague of locusts that devastated parts of northern Italy.

The ecclesiastical view did not necessarily condone cruelty to beasts, a charge often levelled at the philosopher René Descartes (1595–1650). Descartes argued that God had created animals as automata whose actions stemmed solely

A 20th-century depiction of the execution of a sow which was put on trial for infanticide and convicted at Falaise, Normandy, in 1386. Pigs were frequently tried for attacking or killing children in medieval France. Defence counsel for accused animals was provided at public expense.

The owl on the silver four-drachma coin from ancient Athens (below) is a symbol of the city's patron, Athene, the Greek goddess of wisdom, who was goddess of darkness in an earlier incarnation. The owl came to represent wisdom via its more natural link with the dark. It has also been considered a wise animal in many other cultures, because its nocturnal vigilance is associated with that of the studious scholar or wise elder. In Native American belief owls are linked with divination and supernatural knowledge. According to one Christian tradition, the bird represents the wisdom of Christ, which appeared amid the darkness of the unconverted.

REINCARNATION

The question of whether animals possess souls or consciousness is a peculiarly Western issue. In the East, Hindus, Buddhists, Sikhs and Jains believe that the soul is immortal and may be reincarnated within any physical form, human or animal. In Chinese Buddhism a department of Hell was dedicated to assigning new bodies to the souls of the dead. How one was reborn depended on one's *karma*, or balance of virtue and sin: virtuous animals could be reborn as humans.

One Buddhist tale relates how a priest was about to slaughter a goat for a ritual and saw that the creature was chuckling. "Why are you laughing? I am about to kill you!" the priest enquired. The goat replied that it was going to be reborn as a frog. "And that makes you happy?" asked the priest. "No. I am laughing because in my last life I was a priest!"

from their physical construction. They displayed no behaviour (such as the ability to talk or reason) deriving from the existence of a mind or soul, which was unique to humans.

Some intellectuals strongly disagreed with Cartesian doctrine (one theologian even denounced it in 1648 as "murderous") and serious advocacy of a statement of the legal rights of animals began in the 18th century. The central question, in the words of the English philosopher Jeremy Bentham, was "not Can they reason? nor Can they talk? but Can they suffer?" A landmark for animal rights campaigners was the creation in England in 1824 of the Society for the Prevention of Cruelty to Animals or SPCA ("Royal" from 1840), the world's first national animal welfare organization.

Late 20th-century research has furnished startling proof of animal learning abilities. Between 1966 and 1971 US scientists B.T. and R.A. Gardner taught a chimpanzee, Washoe, around 150 words in sign language (ASL). Other chimpanzees have also learned ASL and use it freely to communicate with each other. They have even developed slang, for example using the ASL for "dirty" as an oath.

The widely held notion that only humans (and, to a limited extent, other primates) possess the capacity to employ tools is now generally discredited. A woodpecker finch of the Galapagos Islands (above) wields a twig to "fish" for termite grubs in an old log. Recent studies of insects have shown that ants, for example, will use a piece of soft wood as a sponge to gather moisture.

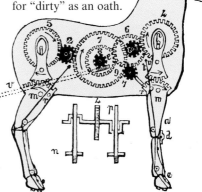

A mechanical horse. According to Descartes, animals were "thoughtless brutes": "Nature acts within them in accordance with the disposition of their organs, in the same way that a clock, which is made up merely of springs and wheels, is able to mark the time of day." Descartes's view was immensely influential and led some to assert that when a beast was hit its howls were only physical reflexes rather than a sign of pain.

Communication

The language of animals has always fascinated humankind. Aristotle noted that the voice of dolphins was very like that of humans, "in that they can pronounce vowels ... but have trouble with consonants". In the 17th century, Montaigne speculated that man's inability to communicate with animals was largely his own fault, so that "they may think us beasts as we think them".

Yet most of the ways that animals communicate among themselves have only recently been discovered, and very few involve making sounds that humans would recognize. Asian elephant herds dispersed through thick jungle keep in touch by clearing their throats at a pitch below the level of human hearing, projecting the sound by using their large, partly hollow foreheads as speakers. Such low-frequency *infrasound* carries further through the bush than would a higher pitch. At the other end of the scale, the 2,000 species of the tiny fruit fly avoid interbreeding because each species has a different courtship song, produced by varying its wing beats. The mosquito also courts by beating its wings. The female produces a hum at a frequency of 500 hertz only when she is ready to mate, a fact discovered in the 19th century when early electrical lighting, operating at this frequency, attracted swarms of male mosquitoes. The male mole cricket also makes its mating call by rubbing its wings together. To ensure it is heard, it digs a burrow with a trumpet-shaped opening which acts as an amplifier. It is so efficient that, just above the burrow, the cricket's mating call registers over 90 decibels, the volume of heavy traffic on a city street.

Long-range communication is often carried out with scents. Animals use scent to mark their territory, issue warnings, "musk" each other to make and reinforce group bonds, or advertise for mates. Humans also communicate with scent, despite their comparatively poor sense of smell (humans have about 0.8 sq inches – 4 sq cm – of olfactory

BEE DANCES

A returning bee communicates the location of flowers it has found to the rest of the hive by dancing. If the flowers are within 300 feet (100m), it performs a circular dance. If the flowers are further away, it does a figure-of-eight dance with a pronounced waggle between the two loops. The dance usually takes place on the vertical comb, and if the waggle is upward the flowers are in the same direction as the sun. The angle of the waggle from the vertical gives the precise direction of the flowers, and the frequency of the waggle tells the other bees the distance to the flowers.

Medieval English beekeeping, illustrated in the 13th-century Ashmole Bestiary.

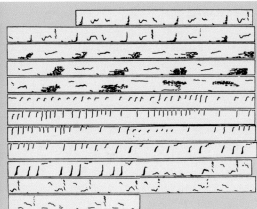

WHALE SONGS

The song of the blue whale is the loudest sound made by any living creature, at 188 decibels exceeding even the roar of a jet engine. However, it is so low that it can hardly be heard by humans, only felt as vibrations. Natural variations in the salinity of sea water make acoustic "corridors", which conduct sound, and by using these it has been estimated that whales can communicate with each other across the breadth of the Pacific Ocean. A single thirty-minute song may contain up to 100 million bits of information. Each species of whale has its own characteristic noise. The piked whale produces a series of regular "thumps", while the mournful whistling that most people identify with whale song is made by the humpback. Within these broad patterns, each individual whale is immediately identifiable by

The humpback whale may breach (left) as courtship behaviour, or simply to remove barnacles from its flanks. The spectrographic recording (right) contains a fragment of a whale song. Each song can last half an hour, and songs may follow each other without break in 22-hour sessions.

its own complex melodies. A whale is constantly modifying its song, and over a period of two years composes a completely new signature tune.

membrane, compared to the 5 sq inches – 150 sq cm – of a small dog). It has been suggested that many apparently irrational likes and dislikes among people are actually subliminal reactions to airborne hormones called *pheromones*.

Animals that can see each other exchange an elaborate range of visual signals. The higher mammals get most information from each other's faces. In general, the more the facial skin is pulled backwards, the more frightened the animal. Dominant animals, even when showing their teeth as a threat,

keep the corners of the mouth pushed forward. Humans have the most expressive faces of all animals, although we share many expressions, including pouting, with the monkeys and apes. Our closeness to the apes has led to various attempts to teach them to talk using sign language, and a gorilla called Koko, at Stanford University, California, seems able to hold conversations. There is heated debate as to whether apes such as this one are really making language, or merely responding to the unwitting cues of their mentors.

Hunting

The first stone tools, found at Hadar in Ethiopia and dated to 2.5 million years ago, indicate that early humans were adept at butchering dead animals for food (the flesh), clothing (the hide) and implements (bones and ivory). However, archaeologists have so far been unable to determine whether these were the tools of hunters or, as seems more probable, scavengers who fed off animals which had fallen prey to other beasts or had been immobilized through natural causes, such as a fall.

The hunting of animals appears to have developed as an essential part of the human way of life only after the larger-brained *Homo erectus* superseded *Homo habilis* about 1.5 million years ago. Over the next 1.3 million years or so the tools of butchery were refined (implying perhaps that the supply of meat was more regular than it could have been through scavenging), and the discovery of several butchered animals of one species in the same place suggests an organized kill rather than a chance find. The first hunters may have endeavoured to reproduce situations in which, as scavengers, they encountered immobilized animals, for example by driving them into swamps or over cliffs.

People proved highly successful hunters because of their ability to anticipate animal behaviour, plan a hunting strategy in advance, and devise sophisticated weapons and traps adapted to each species of prey. Until the invention of firearms the most common hunting weapon in most cultures was the bow and arrow, but other instruments include rocks, spears, blowpipes and clubs. Australian Aboriginal hunters traditionally depend on the boomerang, an aerodynamically sophisticated throwing club (it is heavier and straighter than the boomerang used for sport and display). Many of these weapons are still in use in societies where hunting remains essential, although some peoples, such as the Inuit, have tended to adopt firearms.

As hunters, humans are unique among animals in using other creatures to help catch their prey. The dog was

A 19th-century popular print of a Native American Plains hunter. Horses, introduced to the Americas by the Spanish, reached the Plains around 1600. Over the next two centuries peoples such as the Dakota switched from a predominantly agrarian lifestyle to one based on hunting (a reversal of the usual human trend), prompted by the ease with which horses enabled them to hunt the great herds of bison. This way of life ended in the 19th century when Europeans hunted the animal almost to extinction.

King Assurbanipal of Assyria (669–627BC) killing a lion, from the walls of his palace in Ninevah. Only Assyrian royalty and nobility were allowed to hunt lions, which were caught or bred for the hunt. The Near Eastern lion was finally hunted to extinction in the 19th century.

FALCONRY

The earliest evidence for falconry or hawking, the use of birds of prey to hunt game, comes from 8th-century BC Mesopotamia. European crusaders, travellers and traders in the Near East took the sport to Europe in the Middle Ages and it became a popular aristocratic pursuit. As the name implies, falcons are the most widely employed birds in falconry, but hawks and occasionally eagles are also trained for hunting.

Falconry exploits the predator's ability to swoop swiftly on small mammals and game birds. Falconers use the term "falcon" only of the more intrepid female bird, which is preferred for hunting. The male is one third smaller and is known as a "tiercel". Falconry flourishes today in western Asia and among a small band of specialists in Europe and the USA. In recent years wildlife protection laws have limited the ability of falconers to take young birds for training.

A Saudi falconer with assistants and a saker falcon, which is used to hunt another bird, the bustard.

the first creature to be used in hunting (*c*.12,000BC). Dogs were appreciated for their ability to hunt in packs, to detect and bring down prey, and to warn of danger in the form of wild animals. The use of horses in hunting developed much later, in the Near East: among the first to hunt on horseback were the Hittites and the Babylonians (*c*.1500BC).

The gradual but almost worldwide adoption of farming from *c*.8000BC reduced the human dependence on hunting. But it continued to be an important, if not essential, source of food and was often pursued in order to protect communities and their livestock from wild animals. In some places, such as ancient Egypt, the hunters formed a discrete professional class.

Hunting also persisted as a source of luxury goods, such as furs and ivory, and as a sport it retained an important social function as a means of displaying masculine prowess, especially among royalty and the noble warrior classes. The ancient Romans were untypical in

BULLFIGHTING

Some varieties of hunting developed into spectator sports in which the chase became highly stylized as a gladiatorial combat, usually to the death, between man and animal. The most ancient of these sports is bullfighting, which was popular in ancient Crete and Rome and survives to this day in Spain, Portugal, the south of France and Latin America.

In the modern Spanish bullfight, the main combatant in the bullring is the matador, who uses a cape (below). The chief excitement of each fight lies in the matador's ability to work as close to the horns as possible, which requires great agility if he is not to be gored. The matador wins acclaim for grace and lack of fear and the fight ends when he swiftly dispatches the exhausted animal by thrusting a sword into its neck. After the kill the bull is butchered and distributed among the needy.

A Japanese fighting mastiff in ceremonial garment with its master, a member of a Yakuza or mafia gang. For over 2,000 years humans have used the powerful mastiff to fight bulls, bears or its own species, exploiting the animal's hunting instinct for public spectacle. However, mastiffs are not a naturally aggressive breed.

regarding hunting as a rustic pursuit not befitting the nobility.

Hunting for sport, and the hunting and poaching of animals which are slow to reproduce, such as elephants and whales, encounters much opposition today. Those who are opposed to hunting claim that it is cruel, unnecessary and that it threatens certain species with extinction. European hunters helped wipe out the flightless dodo of Mauritius in the 17th century. At the beginning of the 20th century there were an estimated 500,000 blue whales. Within 90 years, it was feared that fewer than a hundred were left.

Hunters argue that their pursuit serves as a form of pest control (in the case of foxhunting), and that game shooting, which operates strictly controlled seasons and implements breeding programmes, acts in the interest of conservation. It is certainly true that the pheasant, a native of east Asia, became widespread across Europe and North America as a consequence of its introduction as game on large estates.

Another argument made for the continuance of non-essential hunting is that it preserves cultural traditions in predominantly urbanized, industrial societies. For example, hunting remains central to many Native Americans who, living within the world's most developed consumer economy, hardly need to hunt for food. But the Hopi of Arizona, like other peoples, see hunting as an issue of spiritual rather than physical survival. Before embarking on an antelope hunt, the Hopi offer prayers and gifts to the animal which, they believe, responds by allowing itself to be killed. After the kill, the hunters cover the dead antelope with a white blanket and blow smoke over it in an act of gratitude for its life. The Hopi see their hunting rituals as a means of preserving a closeness between humans and the natural world which, in an industrial age, would otherwise rapidly cease to exist.

King George V (left) examines a day's bag of Bengal tigers in India, 1911. Trophies of exotic animals, especially fierce ones, were eagerly amassed by European hunters as symbols both of personal prowess and colonial conquest.

Animals and food

Excavated settlements in the Fertile Crescent of the Middle East, dating from the period more than 10,000 years ago when humans had begun raising crops, but had not yet domesticated animals, reveal a high proportion of fox bones among the leftovers. Within a thousand years people were eating domestic goats and sheep, and a thousand years after that, pigs and cattle. As humans domesticated more animals for food, they seem to have lost their appetite for predators, although dogs are still eaten in parts of the Far East.

It is not known when humans began making cheese from the milk of their livestock, but the Bible mentions "cheese of the herd" being given to King David, and cheesemaking was known to Hesiod, writing in 700BC. Cheese is made from the milk of cows, goats, sheep, yaks, llamas, camels, buffaloes and horses. The goat is a major source of milk in China, Egypt, India and other Asian countries, but the most important milk providers are cows and buffaloes. Whenever blood passes through a cow's udder, some of its components are used to make milk. More than 50 gallons (200 litres) of blood must pass through the udder to make a single pint (0.5 litres) of milk, and a Holstein cow can produce more than 40 pints (80 litres) of milk a day. The energy needed to maintain this vast flow of blood has to come from fresh pasture, supplemented by hay, green crops and silage. In addition, beef cows convert only 4 per cent of what they eat into meat, leading to a situation where a country such as the United States feeds half the grain it grows to its cattle. Poor cultures cannot afford such profligacy, and cattle-rearing peoples, such as the

Of the 277 breeds of cattle, only 18 are solely draft animals. Working cattle are usually oxen – castrated bulls – because of their combination of strength and docility, although cows have also been used, as shown in a 2,000-year-old tomb painting from Thebes (right). In most countries outside Africa or Asia, horses and tractors took over from oxen, and cattle were bred less for strength and more for milk or beef (as shown in the 19th-century painting of a prize bull, above).

Dinka of Sudan or the Masai of Kenya, do not kill their cows. Instead they "tap" their animals' veins for small quantities of blood, which they drink mixed with milk. The cattle seem unperturbed by the bleeding.

Sweetness signified to our ape-like, fruit-eating ancestors that food was ripe and ready to eat, and a sweet tooth is still a common human trait. Beekeeping was one of the first forms of animal husbandry. The ancient Egyptians encouraged wild bees to build their hives in hollow pipes. They often destroyed the pipes and the hives when they took the honey. Although honey was humankind's main source of sugar until the sugar cane boom of the 16th century, it was not until a hundred years later that the role of the queen was properly understood, and smoke was used to pacify angry hives. One of man's surviving, ancient, natural partnerships is with the honeyguide. This small bird whistles to let a member of the Boran tribe of Kenya know that it wishes to lead him to a wild beehive. The man and bird sing to each other throughout the journey to the hive, and after the tribesman has broken in and taken the honey, he leaves a piece of the comb as payment for the bird.

Such mutual cooperation is significantly absent from modern factory farming. As soon as battery chickens leave the egg they are sorted on a conveyor belt according to sex. The males are gassed, while the females have the tips of their beaks removed to stop them mutilating or even cannibalizing themselves, and are loaded into cages that, as they grow, allow them no freedom to move. They are fed by conveyor belt, in constant artificial daylight to keep them laying eggs, which roll from the cage onto another belt. An estimated seven thousand million chickens endure such conditions worldwide.

VEGETARIANISM

The practice of avoiding flesh-eating on a daily basis, rather than as part of some ritual purification, arose simultaneously in India and the Eastern Mediterranean. It is first recorded in the teachings of Pythagoras, around 500BC, but it was Buddhism that spread the doctrine of respect for all living things through India and the Far East.

Vegetarianism received a great impetus in Europe in the 17th and 18th centuries, encouraged by the writings of humanitarian thinkers such as Voltaire and Thoreau, and by Protestant fundamentalist readings of the Bible.

Jainist monks pursue the ideal of ahimsa, *or harmlessness. They do not wash in case they kill organisms on their bodies. They brush the ground where they are about to walk and even wear masks to avoid breathing in insects.*

Performing animals

The earliest records of animals being used as entertainment are wall paintings, dating from 2500BC, excavated on the island of Crete. They show young men and women somersaulting over the backs of charging bulls, being cheered on by large crowds who watch from tiers of raised seating. The use of massive arenas for animal shows peaked – and died out – with the Roman Empire, but wandering Dark Age and medieval minstrel groups would often include performing dogs, dancing bears or liveried monkeys that had been trained to beg for coins. The circus, with its characteristic ring, was invented in 1770 by a British cavalry sergeant, who discovered that centrifugal force would allow him to stand on the back of a horse that was galloping in a circle. In the 19th century, travelling menageries became a necessary adjunct to any successful circus, and in the 1830s the American Isaac Van Amburgh became the first man to put his head in a lion's mouth.

Most animal acts mock their performers. Elephants balance on tiny podiums, and monkeys walk on their hind legs, like caricature humans. It has never been clear how much cruelty is involved in training these animals, and in the face of growing public concern the old-style circuses have largely died out in the USA and Britain, although they thrive in the rest of Europe.

Dolphins and killer whales need no encouragement to perform. The early 20th-century marinelands were barren pools, with only some pebbles on the bottom. In order to amuse themselves, the dolphins would take these pebbles in their mouths and throw them at the visitors. They were especially fond of peppering nuns, probably because the black and white habits reminded them of natural enemies, such as killer whales. When their keepers threw balls and other toys into their pools to distract them, the dolphins began performing tricks spontaneously.

A Victorian children's illustration of the circus.

COMBAT SPORTS

In Bali, cock-fighting is a religious ceremony which takes place in the temples. Two equal-sized birds are matched against each other, with long metal spurs attached to their hind claws to cause maximum damage. The losing bird invariably dies, and its blood is regarded as a sacrifice for a successful harvest. The metal spur is common to most of the countries where cock-fighting still takes place, and was already a part of the sport in Europe by the 12th century. In Thailand, cocks are matched without spurs, and the bird that is losing a fight simply retreats. The Thais also pit bulls and rams against each other in the same way: the animals are not goaded, but fight each other because of their naturally aggressive temperaments, with the loser usually running away and suffering no serious injury.

In the Middle Ages, Britain was notorious

Long after it was banned in Britain, bear-baiting continued clandestinely, as seen in this 1864 Illustrated Sporting News.

among European travellers for its ill-treatment of animals. Badgers, apes, bears and bulls were all frequently tortured, or baited, by dogs which might then be turned on each other.

Every thoroughbred horse in the world can be traced back to three Arab stallions, Darley Arabian, Godolphin Arabian and Byerley Turk, which were imported into England in the early 18th century and crossed with some of the sturdy British breeds. The thoroughbred owes its speed to a heart which can go from 25 beats a minute at rest to more than 250 beats a minute at full gallop. Racehorses are the most valuable animals in the world, regularly fetching millions of dollars at auction, yet this is negligible compared to the amounts wagered on races every day. Betting on which of two or more animals is the faster is one of the oldest and most popular human recreations. Indonesians race bulls and Lapps race reindeer. Greyhounds and pigeons attract massive gambling interest in Europe, as do hermit crabs in East Africa and the Caribbean.

Animals and Belief

Among the first religious or mystically significant rituals for which there is archaeological evidence were those performed in France and Israel by Neanderthals, as much as 70,000 years ago. They consist of buried bodies, laid to rest as if they were asleep, aligned with the rising and setting sun, and surrounded by weapons and the bones of bison, reindeer, boar and other creatures of the hunt. At about the same time, in Switzerland and Germany, giant bear skulls were being arranged and sealed away in crude stone cabinets: the first animal cult for which evidence has survived.

Early humans must have discovered a great deal about how to find food, and what it was safe to eat or to hunt, by observing animals, information which could be codified and passed on through cults and folklore. Native Americans, such as the Athabascans, believed that, long ago, men took beavers, salmon, bears and other creatures as wives, and learned about nature from them: "We have been here thousands of years, and were taught long ago by the animals themselves." This belief encapsulates the first stages in the evolution of animals in the human mind – from teachers to ancestors to protective spirits and finally to gods. It is a measure of the flexibility that made humans so successful that in none of these stages do the animals necessarily stop being prey.

A sacred white cow, decorated for a festival, depicted on a batik painting from Kashmir in India.

Creation and the cosmos

Animals and monsters of cosmic size and significance feature in the creation myths and cosmologies of almost every culture. The most widely occurring image derived from the animal world is that of a great egg floating in the primordial void or waters, from which the elements of the universe, or some creator deity, are hatched. According to Egyptian myth, the supreme sun god emerged from a cosmic egg formed by the union of eight deities representing the forces of chaos. Chinese myth also relates how a creator deity (Pan Gu) came into existence inside a great egg floating in the cosmic void. After 18,000 years the egg burst open and its thick and heavy parts became the earth, while the clear and light elements rose to become the vault of the heavens.

Egg-laying creatures – birds and snakes – figure prominently in myth as cosmic animals. In general, birds represent the higher celestial regions, while snakes, such as Apep, the Egyptian serpent of chaos, stand for the turbulent forces of the earth and the underworld. Birds are especially common in southeast Asian creation stories: for example, the Iban, a tribal people of Borneo, relate how the first beings to exist were two spirits, Ara and Irik, who took the form of birds. They hovered above the infinite cosmic waters, from which they

This 18th-century Indian miniature shows deities and demons using the multi-headed serpent Vasuki as a rope to twist Mount Mandara and churn up the primal ocean, from which emerged the sun, the moon and the elixir of immortality. Vasuki, a king of the Nagas, a race of serpents prominent in Hindu mythology, is sometimes said to bear the world on his heads.

retrieved two eggs, one of which became the sky and the other the earth.

The cosmic serpent as a prime mover in the act of creation is prominent in many cultures. In Hindu myth the god Vishnu is said to rest on the back of the serpent Ananta in the period of the cosmic cycle between the dissolution of one universe and the emanation of the next. From Mali to southern Algeria it is said that the first being made by the creator god was the serpent Minia, whose head was in the sky and whose tail was in the subterranean waters. The god sacrificed Minia and cut its corpse

The ouroboros, the serpent or dragon swallowing its own tail (or emerging from itself), is an almost universal image that occurs, for example, in ancient Greece, Central America and southern Africa. Combining the snake with a circle – the symbol of eternity – the creature represents the endless cosmic cycle of creation and destruction. This ouroboros (left) is from a medieval Greek manuscript on alchemy.

into seven parts, from which he formed the world. Elsewhere in Africa the primal serpent is identified with the rainbow, which is envisaged as a great snake coiled around the earth and holding it together. The "rainbow serpent" also plays a key role in Australian Aboriginal origin myths.

A drawing of a 4,000-year-old Babylonian lapis lazuli seal. The Babylonian god Marduk triumphs over the female dragon Tiamat, the divine embodiment of the forces of chaos. In the beginning Tiamat, the sweet waters, coupled with Apsu, the salt waters, to produce many gods. The young deities rebelled and slew Apsu, but then came under attack from Tiamat. Marduk killed her and, with chaos dead, formed the sky and the earth from her body.

This Easter Island rock painting shows the divine man-bird Make Make, the creator of the universe. In his hand he holds the egg from which the universe was hatched.

TURTLES AND TORTOISES

The legendary strength of the turtle and the tortoise probably accounts for the central roles they play in the creation myths of many peoples. Chinese myth relates how the goddess Nü Gua used the legs of a tortoise to prop up the heavens, and in the Hindu account of the churning of the ocean, Mount Mandara was set on the back of the tortoise Kurma, an incarnation of the god Vishnu. The turtle appears in many Native American accounts as the "earth diver", the animal which retrieved mud from the bed of the primal sea to form the first land. The land grew so heavy that only the turtle could carry it on its back. In the cosmology of the forest peoples of northeastern North America, a Great Tree linking all the regions of the cosmos is said to grow from the back of a primal turtle.

Animals and the gods

In most cultures animals have been linked with the supernatural forces which were believed to control both the natural world and the destiny of humans. As such they have often been revered as the agents and associates of gods and goddesses, or have even become the focus of worship as deities in their own right.

Real and fabulous creatures appear in most mythologies as sacred emblems of gods and goddesses, often embodying particular qualities ascribed to a deity. For example, the bull, a symbol of unpredictable, elemental strength, was associated by the ancient Greeks with the sea-god Poseidon, whose earliest manifestation was as a god of storms. The swan, an attribute of the love goddess Aphrodite, was associated with the ancient motif of the winged phallus: it symbolized both her role as the deity presiding over human sexuality and her unusual birth from the severed genitals of the god Kronos, which fell from heaven into the sea.

Many deities have animal companions and familiars. Foxes are the messengers of the Japanese rice god Inari, and two of the animals stand at the entrance to the god's shrines. In Hinduism the most famous exemplar is probably the monkey god Hanuman, the chief disciple of the god Rama. Hanuman's selfless dedication to Rama is seen as a paradigm of the intimacy that can exist between deity and devotee. Other animals associated with individual Hindu deities also carry great symbolic importance. The celestial goose Hamsa, the mount of the creator god Brahma, embodies the spirit of cre-

THE CAT CULT

The worship of felines in ancient Egypt centred on two goddesses who are often regarded as contrasting aspects of a single deity: the lion-headed Sekhmet and the cat-headed Bastet. The ferocious Sekhmet, daughter of the creator sun god Ra, was venerated as a protector of the universe who warded off evil spirits, disaster and plague. Bastet, however, was a benign deity associated with motherhood, love and fertility (she was often represented with kittens). Originally a lion-headed goddess, she came to be depicted as a cat *c*.2000BC, about 500 years before the appearance of the domestic animal. The cat's role as a fertility deity may have derived from the perception that the (subsequently domesticated) feral cat was a protector of grain, because it killed the rodents which infested granaries.

A cat mummy from Abydos, c.200BC. Domesticated cats were revered as representatives of the goddess Bastet and, although it was a crime to kill them, thousands were buried in cemeteries sacred to the goddess.

A bronze statuette of the Late Period (664–332BC) depicting Bastet. Her cult centred on Bubastis (modern Tell Basta) in the Nile delta, where a spring festival was held in her honour.

ation. Makara, a hybrid monster that is the vehicle of the god Varuna, is the spirit of the waters. Garuda, part eagle and part human, is the mount of Vishnu and the destroyer of evil, especially in the form of serpents.

Divinities are often believed to possess the ability to manifest themselves in the form of an animal. For example, in Irish myth, war goddesses such as Badhbh and the Morrigán were said to hover over battlefields in the form of a crow or raven (carrion birds which are seen in many cultures as omens or emblems of death) and alight on the corpses of slain warriors.

In the pre-Columbian civilizations of Central and South America, gods were often portrayed wearing the jaguar's skin as a sacred costume, and the cat was venerated as the divine protector of royalty by both Maya and Aztec rulers. Tezcatlipoca ("Lord of the Smoking Mirror"), the supreme Aztec god and the patron deity of royalty, was said to possess an animal alter ego in the form of a great jaguar which inhabited the summits of mountains and the entrances to caves.

According to Hindu mythology the first three avatars (incarnations) of Vishnu were Kurma the tortoise, Varaha the boar and Narasimha the man-lion. In Greek myth, the god Zeus metamorphosed into an animal to accomplish some of his most notable seductions and abductions. He turned into a bull to kidnap a beautiful princess, Europa, seduced Leda, the queen of Sparta, in the form of a swan, and became an eagle to snatch the handsome prince Ganymede and carry him to Mount Olympus. In these myths the animal symbolism is unlikely to be accidental: the bull embodies virility and male power, the swan is phallic and the

eagle represents apotheosis and the power of the heavens (an eagle was said to carry the thunderbolts that were the chief weapons of Zeus).

Many Egyptian deities were partly or wholly animal in form, and the nature of the animal was generally reflected in the character of the god or goddess. For example, the sky goddess Nut was sometimes portrayed as a sow. Just as a sow will sometimes eat its young, Nut was said to swallow the sun every night. Anubis, the god of mummies who conducted the souls of the dead into the underworld, was frequently depicted as a man with the head of a jackal, a scavenger that was believed to haunt the cemeteries.

The divine culture heroes and tricksters of Native

The antelope is widely associated with the moon and fecundity. According to the Bambara people of Mali, the creator god Faro sent a divine antelope, represented by this wooden sculpture, down to earth to teach agriculture to humans.

American tradition are anthropomorphic in nature and are said to switch between their animal and human forms. Thus the trickster-hero Raven is envisaged both as a raven with human attributes, such as the ability to talk, and as a man with supposed raven attributes, such as greed, and in myth it is sometimes difficult to discern which, if either, is intended. These animal-human deities are greatly venerated as clan founders and as the spirits which preside over important aspects of Native American ceremonial. For example, Coyote is the protective deity of the Navaho curing ceremony Coyoteway, which is performed to treat those who fall ill with "Coyote sickness". This is said to arise when a person disrupts his or her harmonious relationship with the divinity, for example by killing a coyote. In the course of the ceremony, another member of the tribe assumes the guise and identity of Coyote and helps to restore the state of harmony and thus cure the illness.

The North American clan spirits are part of a worldwide phenomenon called totemism, in which a natural object such as an animal or plant has kinship with a group of people, or an individual, and is an emblem of that group, or person. The word "totem" comes from the language of the Algonkian-Ojibwa people of the Great Lakes region of North America. It was introduced into English in 1791, specifically and wrongly to mean a guardian spirit. The original term, *ototeman*, meant "his brother-sister kin". According to the Ojibwa, the Great Spirit had given totems to the clans as a reminder that group members were related and could not marry among themselves.

Totemism takes different forms worldwide, but the avoidance of incest is a theme common to many of them. Totemic animals are often seen as progenitors of the group – they must not be eaten, or harmed – and a totem may be inherited patrilineally or matrilineally, depending on the culture. In 1912, the sociologist Emile Durkheim claimed to have found the origins of religion – through the sacralization of emotions that underlie social interactions – in totemism. Others deny that totemism exists, except as a more or less arbitrary way of dividing up societies.

A stylized eagle from the treasure buried with a pagan Anglo-Saxon king at Sutton Hoo in Suffolk, England, c. AD625–50. The eagle was a symbol of the god Woden, the chief deity of the early Germanic pantheon, known elsewhere as Wodan or Odin. He was associated with the heavens, the underworld, magic and warfare. In Norse mythology, Odin took the shape of an eagle to retrieve the mead of divine inspiration, one of the treasures of the gods, after it had been stolen by giants. Other forms of the god were the serpent (symbolic of the underworld) and the wolf and raven (creatures of the battlefield).

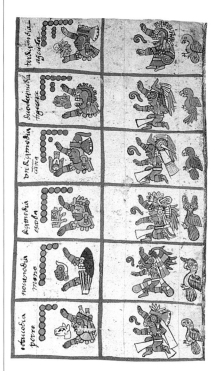

FLIGHT AND THE AZTEC CALENDAR

The Aztec week or *trecena* consisted of thirteen days, each of which had a patron divinity which was in turn associated with a sacred winged creature, or "volatile". Some species have not been identified with certainty:

Day	Divinity	Volatile
1	Xiuhtecuhtli	Hummingbird
2	Tlaltecuhtli	Hummingbird
3	Chalchiuhtlicue	Dove
4	Tonatiuh	Quail
5	Tlazolteotl	Raven
6	Mictlantecuhtli	Owl
7	Cinteotl	Butterfly
8	Tlaloc	Eagle
9	Quetzalcoatl	Turkey
10	Tezcatlipoca	Horned Owl
11	Chalmecatecuhtli	Scarlet Macaw
12	Tlahuizcalpantecuhtli	Quetzal
13	Citlalincue	Parrot

Part of the Book of Days in the Aztec manuscript known as the Codex Borbonicus (c. AD 1520), showing gods of the day and their associated volatiles. Day 13 (Parrot) is at the top, day 8 (Eagle) at the bottom.

The bull was revered from at least the time of the Minoan civilization (c. 1400–1100 BC) as a symbol of divine potency. This frieze from the Parthenon in Athens (built 447–438 BC) shows a bull about to be sacrificed in honour of the goddess Athene. The sacrifice took place at the climax of the annual Great Panathenaia, the greatest of the Athenian religious festivals, during which important citizens brought animals from all over the city's territories to offer to their patron deity.

Animal guardians

Real and fabulous animals play an important role in myth and folklore as guardian spirits. The dragon, perhaps the most widespread of all tutelary beasts, was the protector and symbol of the emperors of China, and was a guardian of royal and national sovereignty in Celtic and Germanic traditions. Elsewhere, big cats are seen as the guardians of kings: this role is fulfilled principally by the lion in Europe, Africa and the East, and by the jaguar in Central and South America.

Animals may be revered as the protectors of humanity in general. In Native American myth, figures such as

In this Egyptian papyrus of c.1250BC the jackal-headed god of embalming, Anubis, weighs the heart (that is, the soul) of the scribe Ani against the feather of truth. Anubis was the guardian of the dead, whom he guided into the underworld for judgment before the god Osiris.

Raven and Coyote use cunning rather than ferocity to protect humans from monsters and other perils. The Yeti of Himalayan legend are sometimes said to be guardian spirits associated with Chen-re-zi, the Buddhist god of mercy.

Animals are frequently seen as sacred guardians of life force, especially in shamanistic cultures: a shaman often draws curing and visionary powers

CLAN GUARDIANS

In Native American traditions of the northwest coastal region, anthropomorphic animal figures are revered as clan founders, helpers and spirit guardians. These figures, who include Raven, Blue Jay, Bear, Mink and Eagle, are

A house partition screen of c.1840. It depicts a brown bear, the clan guardian of Chief Shakes of the Tlingit people of southern Alaska.

depicted on totem poles and artefacts as heraldic clan emblems. The "portal pole" in front of a clan house has an opening which symbolizes the gateway to the spirit world, over which the carved figure of the clan ancestor stands guard. An encounter with the ancestor is central to many rituals such as the Kwakiutl *hamatsa*, an initiation into a secret medicine society. The initiate enters a trance, during which the animal ancestor appears.

from an animal spirit who acts as his or her personal protector and guide in the spirit world. In Christian tradition the stag and unicorn, symbols of Christ, are said to guard the tree of life.

Fearsome animals that keep watch over sacred places and the gateways to spirit worlds also warn of the dangers of passing into the regions of the unknown. In Greek myth the monstrous three-headed dog Cerberus guarded the mouth of the underworld, barring the living from entering and the dead from leaving. Medieval European artists sometimes depicted the entrance to Hell as the jaws of a dragon.

Beasts frequently protect repositories of wealth, both physical (treasure) and spiritual (wisdom or secret lore). European mythic traditions often present a human hero, such as the Greek Jason and the Germanic Sigurd and Beowulf, in conflict with a dragon to win a hoard of treasure. The Greek Sphinx was a keeper of hidden wisdom who killed those who failed to answer her riddle. More benign are the lion-dogs of Fo, revered in Chinese Buddhism as guardians of the law and symbols of the enlightenment of the Buddha.

The winged protective spirit occurs frequently in Babylonian culture: this bull-man stood at the entrance to the palace of King Sargon of Assyria (who ruled 721–705 BC) at Khorsabad. It appears to have five legs, but this is in fact an artistic device. The statue is meant to appear as if it is standing when viewed from the front, but striding when seen from the side.

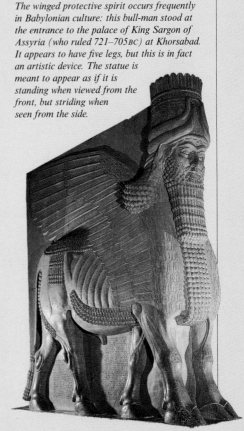

Animal tricksters

Myth and folklore often credit animals with the human qualities suggested by various aspects of their behaviour. Swift and agile creatures with the ability to outmanoeuvre bigger and more dangerous beasts appear as tricksters, characters whose joking, mischievous or stupid behaviour subverts the ordered world. The trickster is typically depicted as a greedy thief, like the popular Chinese mythological character of Monkey, who has the whole hierarchy of heaven in furious pursuit after gorging himself on the peaches of immortality which are strictly reserved for the gods and buddhas.

Among the anthropomorphic animal divinities of Native American tradition, the Raven is particularly renowned as a trickster thief. For example, the Blackfoot of western Canada relate how Raven stole all the buffaloes, antelope, deer, moose and rabbits, so that people had nothing to hunt and began to starve. The creator god Old Man turned himself into a dog and, with the assistance of a chief's son, found all the game animals hidden in a cave and released them. But when the people attempted to drive a herd of buffaloes

An 18th-century engraving illustrating one of Aesop's fables. The fox tricks the raven by flattering him so much that he cannot resist agreeing with the compliment – and drops the cheese in his beak as soon as he speaks. The wily fox is well known in European folk myth, most notably in the medieval figure of Reynard.

Spiders are widely admired for the apparent ingenuity and patience they display in building webs or, like the wolf spider (left), burrows. In the mythology of the Azande and other peoples of West and Central Africa, the spider is a trickster figure who regularly outwits elephants, lions and monsters.

over a cliff (an ancient method of hunting), Raven suddenly appeared and drove them back from the cliff edge. This was the last straw: Old Man caught Raven, hung him over a fire as punishment and then ordered him to mend his selfish ways.

The activities of the animal trickster are not always negative in effect, and often the creature embodies the qualities of a culture hero, a creator figure who helps to form the ordered world and furthers the interests of humanity, often in opposition to the gods. For instance, the Dogon of Mali relate how Pale Fox used his cunning to steal seeds from the creator god Amma and bring agriculture to humans.

However, probably the most important task carried out by the animal trickster-hero is the theft of fire, an episode which is recounted in one form or another in most mythologies of the world. These stories commonly follow a basic pattern, in accordance with which an often very small animal trickster outwits the more powerful (even divine) keeper of fire. In a myth told in the Andaman Islands of the Indian Ocean, for example, Kingfisher steals fire from a great creator-ancestor figure called Biliku. Similarly, the San (Bushmen) of the Kalahari desert attribute the acquisition of fire to Mantis, who stole it

*The coyote (*Canis latrans*) or prairie wolf is renowned as a trickster from Alaska to Costa Rica, playing a role akin to that of the fox in Old World tradition. The creature is said to have a vast appetite (it is an omnivorous animal): in one myth Coyote changes into a dish so that he can be piled high with food. The real coyote has tricks of its own, such as playing dead to attract its prey, which it then pounces on.*

from Ostrich, and the Ila of Zambia claim that the mason wasp brought fire to earth from God.

Sometimes a creature's twin roles of trickster and culture hero are kept distinct: for example, the Tlingit people of Alaska acknowledge two Raven figures, one disruptive and the other creative.

Many accounts of the antics of trickster animals are primarily intended to be absurd or humorous in effect, especially when the trickster dupes himself or otherwise receives a taste of his own medicine. For example, one myth of the Winnebago people of Wyoming and Nebraska relates how Coyote's arms had a fight with each other while he was skinning a buffalo with a sharp knife. The animal ended up with painfully gashed arms and ruing his own stupidity for allowing such a thing to happen.

RABBITS AND HARES

Rabbits and hares (*Leporidae*) are among the most nimble, alert and prolific of all mammals – a female rabbit can have 50 offspring a year – and occur as tricksters in the mythology of every region where they are indigenous.

They are typically portrayed as underdogs who rely on ingenuity and athleticism to get the better of creatures which are often their

natural predators, such as the hyena (in African myth) and the wolf (in North America). For example, the Creek people of the southeastern USA tell how Rabbit and Wolf loved the same woman, but she preferred the

handsome Wolf. One day the suitors both went courting and Rabbit, feigning sickness, persuaded Wolf to let him ride on his back. As Rabbit had foreseen, the sight of him riding no less a mount than Wolf so impressed the woman that she agreed to marry him.

The character of Brer Rabbit, brought to the USA in the tales of African slaves, was even able to outwit other typical folkloric trickster figures, such as Brer Fox.

Animals in the sky

From the earliest times the heavens have played a central role in human culture as a distant supernatural domain, the home of the gods and of the celestial counterparts of earthly creatures. Sky animals have been observed in individual heavenly bodies and in the patterns formed by star groups, with strikingly similar perceptions occurring in widely different cultures. For example, the "face" of the moon was traditionally said by both the Chinese and the Aztecs to represent a hare, while the Big Dipper or Plough, part of the constellation known in the West as Ursa Major (Great Bear), is called the Celestial Bear by Native Americans.

Most peoples developed the concept of stellar divination (astrology) based on a zodiac (from Greek *zodiakos kyklos*, "animal circle"), a belt of 12 constellations traversed by the sun on its apparent annual course around the earth (see right). According to Western astrology eight of the constellations represent animals, both real and fabulous, for example the goat-fish Capricornus and the Centaur. In the Chinese zodiac they are all animals, six wild and six tame. These star groups were believed to exercise a controlling influence on the earth at the time when they were visible in the night sky. For example, in Western astrology those born during the appearance of the constellation of the lion (Leo) were said to be proud, fiery and independent, qualities traditionally ascribed to the beast itself. Similar qualities were attributed by the Aztecs to people born under the constellation of the Jaguar.

Animals were central to the astrology of the Incas, who perceived that every species of animal and bird possessed a

twin in the stars which protected and sustained its earthly counterpart. These celestial creatures also exercised a tutelary influence over the fertility and prosperity of the earth: for example, Yacana, the Llama, was said to prevent flooding by drinking excess water from the earth. Similar perceptions persist among present-day Andeans and the tribal peoples of Amazonia, where, for example, the constellation Caterpillar Jaguar is believed to oversee the procreation of caterpillars, an important part of the aboriginal diet of the region.

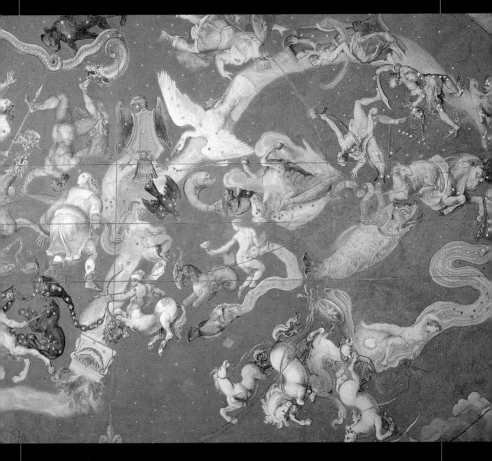

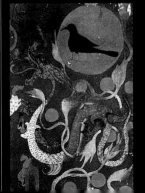

LEFT *According to one Chinese tradition, the soul of the sun takes the form of a crow or raven, as depicted in this Han dynasty silk shroud of c.150BC. It has been suggested that the idea of the solar bird arose from the observation of sunspots by early Chinese astronomers. For example, a 2nd-century AD treatise remarked that for several months in AD118 the sun appeared russet-coloured, and bore a dark shadow "resembling a magpie".*

ABOVE *The ceiling of the late 16th-century Palazzo Farnese at Caprarola, Italy, depicting the 48 constellations then known (there are now 88) and first charted by Ptolemy of Alexandria (c.AD127–145). Most represent beasts, many of them mythological, such as the Hydra and Centaur (bottom left). Ptolemy said that every land was ruled by a constellation: for example, India by Capricornus (goat-fish), Italy by Leo (lion) and Britain by Aries (ram).*

Energy and transformation

Animals figure extensively in mythology and folklore both as guardians and as incarnations of supernatural forces. For example, the dragon embodied the most powerful forces of the earth and heavens. A dragon was one of the emblems of Osiris, the Egyptian god of the underworld: the dragon was said to rise and cause the annual flooding of the Nile, upon which the fertility of the land depended. According to Greek myth, dragons drew the chariot of the fertility goddess Demeter who brought the skills of agriculture to the peoples of the earth. In China dragons were said to inform the landscape: for example, a chain of hills might be a dragon's spine. No new building would be erected before a master of Feng Shui (Chinese geomancy or earth divination) had determined its best position in relation to the energy of local dragons. Feng Shui is still widely practised in Taiwan and Hong Kong and in other Chinese communities outside China.

Many cultures believe that the human soul transmigrates after death into the body of an animal. The Aztecs revered hummingbirds as the transformed souls of dead warriors. Similar beliefs are found in Africa, where the San (Bushmen) believe that after death a hunter becomes an eland. Among the Azande of west-central Africa, a man is said to possess two souls, one of which becomes a totemic animal when he dies.

According to one Buddhist tradition the yeti of Himalayan myth is a creature through which an individual's soul passes after death. It is said to be a beast which hovers between the human and animal worlds: some who claim to have seen it have described it as "more than ape, less than human".

Animals are often linked with parts of the human body or spirit. This association is most highly developed in India, where Minaraja, the 4th-century AD founder of Hindu astrology, first elaborated the notion of *Kalapurusha* or "Time Man". According to Minaraja, the signs of the zodiac were positioned in the heavens on the body of this giant cosmic being: for example, Tavuru (Taurus) the bull was his face and neck. Each of the zodiac beasts also governed the parallel region of the human body, and the characteristics of each creature could be drawn upon by yogic disciplines aimed at the relevant part of the body.

The serpent is widely regarded as phallic and is associated with sexual energy, partly from its shape and partly from its association with the fertility of the earth in which it dwells. In one area of Papua New Guinea, for example, the ancestral culture hero Sida is characterized by a long penis which behaves independently of its owner and may be mistaken for a snake.

A wooden and painted plaster image of a Ba *bird, c.332–330BC. In ancient Egyptian belief a person's spiritual nature or* Ba *was transformed into a bird after his or her death. The* Ba *flew freely through the underworld, the land of the dead, and was able to revisit the earth by day.*

In Greek myth there are many accounts of humans being transformed into animals and birds, often because they have offended the gods. The kingfisher, it was said, was originally the princess Halcyone, who was turned into a bird as a punishment for her presumption in calling herself Hera, the name of the queen of heaven. Aeolus, the king of the winds, took pity on her and once a year calmed the water so that she could hatch her eggs in peace.

ABOVE *Apollo and the Dragon, from the wrought iron gate of the Chelsea Physic Garden, London, made in 1634. The ancient Greeks believed that a great concentration of earth energy issued from a rock crevice at Delphi in south-central Greece, which was said to be the centre of the earth. This power was embodied in the dragon, Python, which was set to guard the sacred site by Gaia, the goddess of the earth. When Apollo, the god of prophecy, light and healing, chose Delphi as his shrine he fought and killed the dragon, which was said to lie buried beneath a stone, the Omphalos ("Navel"), which marked the earth's centre.*

KUNDALINI

The Hindu practice of *kundalini* ("serpent") yoga is an attempt to fuse within one human body the energies of two opposed principles: sexuality (the male principle, or *shiva*) and spirituality (the female principle, or *shakti*). Together *shiva* and *shakti* make up the whole of Reality. *Shakti* is conceived of as a coiled serpent which sleeps at the base of the pelvis between the genitals and the anus. The serpent's mouth is open over the entrance to *sushumna*, the central energy channel which is said to run from the base of the spine to the *sahasrara*, envisaged as a 1,000-petalled lotus at the top of the head. This lotus is pure consciousness, the body's highest energy centre, where *shiva* resides. *Kundalini* yoga aims to awaken the serpent, and draw it up the *sushumna* channel to the lotus, thus uniting body and spirit.

Through breath control and concentration, the *kundalini* adept aims to generate an inner heat in order to rouse the serpent. It is then drawn upward to *sahasrara*, where it stays briefly before returning to *sushumna*. The adept repeats the process until the serpent remains in *sahasrara*, at which point the adept attains the desired state of bliss.

Soul flight

Birds have been seen in most cultures as physical and spiritual intermediaries between the human world and that of the heavens. In Hindu mythology, for example, Garuda, the divine mount of the god Vishnu, is sometimes depicted as part human and part eagle. If a Siberian Evenk shaman wished to fly to the spirit realm, he would use four carved wooden birds: an eagle to protect his soul from evil spirits, a raven to guard him during trance, a swan to carry him to his destination, and a woodpecker, which had the power of healing (a shaman would often travel to the spirit realm in order to recover the lost or kidnapped soul of a sick person). Instead of riding on the back of a swan, a Siberian Nganasan shaman who wished to visit the spirit world could transform himself into a loon, an Arctic diving bird whose otherworldly, guttural sounds and eerie, wailing cries gave rise to its popular name.

Heavenly birds can be the keepers of divine or esoteric wisdom. In imperial China the appearance of the Feng Huang or Chinese phoenix heralded the birth of a great philosopher. Birds are sometimes said to have a language of their own which humans understand only in special circumstances. In Irish myth the hero Finn understood bird language after he ate a magic salmon.

Birds may also represent the flight of the human soul between the worlds of

A painted woodcarving in the malanggan *style from Papua New Guinea, representing a sky being. Birds often figure in the mythology of Melanesia and Micronesia as intermediaries between the human world and the skies. In one story, a hunter shot a bird of paradise which flew off with his arrow. The hunter followed and came to a path that led to the sky. At the end of the path was a village, where the bird of paradise lived in the form of a man.*

the dead and the living. According to Navaho myth, the soul after death assumes the form of an owl, and the souls of dead Amazonian tribespeople may take the form of hummingbirds.

Among the Siberian Yakut, the story is told of a man who died, but could hear everything that was happening around him. When he was buried, he heard a rumbling from the centre of the earth and a black bull came to fetch him. When they arrived at the underworld, however, an old man told the bull to take the corpse back, as he was due to be reborn. After being deposited back on the earth, the corpse was picked up by a raven and carried through a hole in roof of the world to a land where the sun and moon shone together, occupied by people with ravens' heads. There, he was put in a nest at the top of an unimaginably tall larch, and suckled by a winged white reindeer until he was ready to be reborn as a great shaman.

Like the bull in the Yakut story, animals other than birds can be chosen as the vehicles of soul flight. A Siberian

Ibises, from an Egyptian papyrus of the 19th dynasty (1295–1186BC). The ibis was widely venerated and was sacred to the moon god Aah, who was often depicted with an ibis's head. The bird was thought to be free from illness.

Chukchi shaman may ride to the spirit world on the back of a reindeer. When a Canadian Inuit shaman wants to fly, he transforms himself into a polar bear because, when seen swimming through clear water, a polar bear's movements make it look like it is flying.

THE THUNDERBIRD

In Native American mythology great creative and destructive power is attributed to the Thunderbird, a gigantic bird resembling an eagle which is the spirit of the thunderstorm. Thunderclaps are the beating of the bird's wings and lightning is believed to flash from its eyes and beak. Anything struck by the creature's lightning is said to possess particularly strong spiritual power which, according to local tradition, may either be shunned or revered.

In the west there are said to be four Thunderbirds, one inhabiting each of the corners of the world. In the tradition of the Iroquois of the northeast, Thunderbird appears in human guise as guardian of the heavens.

Birds are often linked to elemental powers. The myths of southern Africa tell of a Lightning Bird, and any stones found at a spot where lightning has struck are said to be its eggs.

A Thunderbird eagle on a totem pole from British Columbia. In this region the Thunderbird is said to prey on whales, which it carries off in its talons.

Rock art

Animals feature prominently in the earliest known examples of human art, the paintings produced by early European *Homo sapiens sapiens* between 35,000 to 12,000 years ago in caves and rock shelters in southwestern France and northern Spain. The artistic quality of the prehistoric paintings at sites such as Altamira (discovered 1879) and Les Trois Frères (discovered 1914) has long been recognized.

The artists evidently painted by the light of small tallow lamps (many have been found at Lascaux), and in a number of cases must have constructed scaffolding in order to work in otherwise inaccessible areas close to the cave roof. Paintings made in these positions would have been difficult to view, which has led most authorities to conclude that they were not simply decorative but possessed some more specialized, possibly spiritual, purpose. The majority of the paintings depict the larger types of animal known to the artists, such as deer, bison, horses, and extinct species such as the aurochs (wild ox), woolly rhinoceros, mammoth and cave lion. Occasionally the beasts carry markings which indicate wounds or blood, suggesting some connection with hunting. According to one theory the paintings represent a form of "sympathetic magic", whereby the prehistoric hunters believed that by depicting a beast, they would capture its soul and draw it to its death in the hunt.

People are portrayed infrequently, and usually more sketchily than beasts. They often appear to be wearing animal masks, perhaps an indication that the caves were used for rituals led by a

shamanistic "beastmaster" figure who acted as the intermediary between the human and animal spirit world. Some of these masked "shamans" have an erect penis, which suggests a connection with fertility rites, possibly designed to ensure the abundance of the hunted herds. Smaller animals such as rabbits, which were unlikely to be in short supply, are not portrayed.

Some authorities have proposed that the paintings are what anthropologists call trophy arrays, representing notable kills. If this is the case, the art may have been produced as part of rituals marking a successful hunt.

LASCAUX

In September 1940 four youths discovered a deep shaft in woods near the Dordogne village of Montignac. At the bottom of the shaft they found a sequence of caves containing a spectacular repository of prehistoric art, unseen for thousands of years. The artists used black, yellow, red and brown pigments to produce well-observed depictions of creatures including aurochs, red deer and horses. In a section called the Rotunda (or "Hall of the Bulls") a frieze of aurochs and other beasts includes the largest prehistoric painted figures in the Western world. Elsewhere, in the least accessible area of the caves, a "shaman" or hunter wearing a bird mask appears to confront a bison that has been disembowelled with a spear.

Body heat, moisture from human breath, and bright lights caused the vivid colours to fade and prompted the growth of fungus on the paintings. In 1963 the authorities closed the caves to the public, but a replica of part of the caves (including most of the paintings) was built and opened nearby in 1984.

The aurochs, foal and stag, were painted 17,000 years ago in the rock corridor at Lascaux known as the Axial Gallery.

Hunter and hunted

An intimate spiritual relationship often exists between humans and their prey, based upon the simple fact that the perpetuation of the hunter's life depends directly upon the animal's readiness to concede its own. In such circumstances the hunt becomes a sacrificial bargain between hunter and animal, in which, as the mythologist Joseph Campbell expressed it, "the beast to be slaughtered is interpreted as a willing victim, or rather, as a knowing participant in a covenanted sacred act".

Particular animals may be treated with special reverence by the hunter in order to ensure their continued consent to this covenant. For example, among hunting peoples of the American and Eurasian subarctic the bear is traditionally important as the chief of the game animals, because of its perceived closeness as a species to humanity (see p.76). A bear kill is often conducted with great ceremony aimed at showing gratitude to the creature for letting the hunters take its meat and pelt, in order to ensure that the bear's spirit will be

happy to return within a new body to be hunted again. When the Koryaks of Siberia kill a bear the women endeavour to appease its spirit by dancing in its skin, entreating the animal not to be angry and making it an offering of food. The hunters of the Mackenzie River region in northwest Canada sing to a dying bear to please it and ensure that it will encourage many more bears

Among the Gilyaks of northeast Siberia the bear hunt culminates in a feast at which the bear, attending as guest of honour, is served his own flesh. Similar ceremonies exist among the Ainu of Japan.

Inuit walrus hunters of Greenland. In Inuit belief, seals and walruses were originally the severed fingers of the Sea Spirit, who keeps all game beasts at the bottom of the sea, whence she sends them to be hunted for food and fur.

There are numerous theories about this figure, known as "The Sorcerer", and painted in the caves of Les Trois Frères, France, c.12,000BC. He incorporates the parts of several different animals, but is clearly human. He may be a shaman impersonating a totemic game beast, or a spirit "Master of Animals".

SHAMAN RITES

In hunter societies the religious and ritual aspects of hunting are usually centred on the shaman, who acts as a medium between this world and that of the spirits who control the supply and well-being of game animals. When the hunters of the group require his or her help, the shaman goes into a ritual trance (often induced by hallucinogenic substances or intense rhythmic drum-beating) and his or her soul enters the supernatural domain in an attempt to find the source of difficulty. For example, the shaman may be asked to locate a particular animal or to discover where the spirits have put all the game beasts. (This concern occurs frequently in Native American myths which recount how the game animals were stolen or hidden by a figure of the spirit world, such as the trickster Raven.)

It is often believed that entranced shamans adopt the form and nature of an animal alter ego in order to enhance their effectiveness in securing game for hunters. In Central and South America shamans are said to become jaguars, the most resourceful of natural predators.

to allow themselves to be caught.

The eland, the largest species of antelope, occupies a central position in the mythology and hunting lore of the San (Bushmen) of the Kalahari desert. The animal is said to have been the first thing that was made by the supreme creator being who is often referred to as Mantis. The eland is associated with the moon and female fecundity and is believed to exercise control over the fertility

The San bowman hunts with light, flightless arrows. The relative inaccuracy of these weapons, even in the hands of the skilful San, puts a premium on stealth and tracking.

and prosperity of the group, through its own death and consumption. It is consequently treated with particular reverence, to the extent that, after shooting an eland with arrows dipped in slow-working poison, the San hunter enters into a mystic spiritual union with the dying animal. The poison may take up to a day to cause the creature's death, in which time the hunter observes numerous rites and taboos which, it is believed, hasten the death of his victim.

The concept of the immortal animal soul is widespread among hunting peoples. For example, Alaskan Inuit communities hold annual festivals at the climax of which the inflated bladders of animals killed in the previous twelve months are pushed through holes in the ice. In doing so the hunters believe that they are returning the souls of their prey to the spirit world, whence they will be sent out once more as quarry for Inuit hunters.

Hunting ritual may be focused on communication with a "Master (or Mistress) of Animals", a powerful spirit who controls the souls of game beasts. In return for sacrifices and obedience to certain moral rules, this figure is believed to send animals out to be killed by hunters. Desana shamans from the Amazon even negotiate the exchange of human souls for animal souls. Usually they offer the souls of neighbouring tribes.

The heraldic bestiary

Heraldry is believed to have arisen in northern France in the early 12th century as an easy means of identification in battle and tournaments. However, it subsequently developed into an elaborate symbolic language which was widely used in various non-military contexts to express the social status, character and aspirations of the bearer of a heraldic device.

The lyon-poisson ("lion-fish") is one of numerous hybrids in the heraldic menagerie. Its symbolism is drawn from each of its component creatures: it represents the power of the ocean and fortitude at sea.

Animal and bird symbolism featured prominently in heraldry from the earliest times. Mythical beasts such as the dragon, griffin and two-headed eagle occur almost as much as real creatures, which in many cases take forms that bear little resemblance to their true appearances. Heraldic animals were exploited for their traditional symbolic values or legendary characteristics, many of which were described in the medieval bestiaries. For example, the heraldic leopard or "lybbard" (which is generally identical in appearance with the heraldic lion) represents vigilance, courage and impetuosity. Similarly, fidelity and friendship are symbolized by a heraldic dog. In armorial bearings the type of dog represented is often the talbot, a now extinct English breed of hunting hound that was popular among the aristocracy in the Middle Ages.

On the escutcheon, the heraldic shield which is the essential central element in any armorial bearing (or coat of arms), animals are generally depicted facing *dexter* (to the right of the person

Among the most common heraldic animals, the stag or hart represents male prowess. It stands for the pious believer, symbolism which is derived from the opening verse of Psalm 42: "As the hart panteth after the water brooks, so panteth my soul after thee, O God."

The animal is also an emblem of Jesus Christ: according to a myth recounted in medieval bestiaries, the stag sucked snakes from the ground and devoured them, as Christ overcame the great Serpent (the Devil). The heraldic stag is usually represented as a red deer but the male of numerous species, such as fallow deer, roe deer, reindeer and elk, are also often depicted.

An ancient emblem of nobility, strength and courage, the lion is the oldest of all heraldic beasts. The lion rampant (rearing up defiantly on its hind legs, below) was the original form: other postures were developed later, such as passant (walking past the beholder), guardant (looking full face at the beholder), reguardant (looking behind), statant (standing) and couchant (lying down). As the king of the beasts, the lion (referred to as a "lybbard" or "leopard") frequently occurs as the emblem of monarchy: for example, three lions passant guardant represent the monarch of England and a single lion rampant represents the monarch of Scotland.

HERALDIC FORMS

The early heraldic artists needed little guidance to draw familiar European animals such as the talbot dog or red deer, but it was a different story when they were faced with more exotic creatures. Like the artists who produced the medieval bestiaries (whose work they doubtless consulted) they had to go on hearsay, legend and, at best, second-hand reports, often with curious results. The heraldic leopard, for example, is spot-less, with a mane and bushy-ended tail like a lion's. The panther

The heraldic pelican was usually shown "in her piety", nourishing her chicks with her own blood. The bird was a symbol of Christ, who shed His blood for humanity.

frequently has the talons of an eagle and appears to be exhaling fire (the bestiaries claimed that its breath had powerful properties). The heraldic tiger resembled a lion or even a wolf, often with canine tusks and a horn on its nose. When the real animal became known it was adopted into heraldry under the name "Bengal tiger" to avoid confusion with the traditional heraldic animal.

As in the bestiaries, the pelican was often depicted as a hawk, perhaps an obvious form for a bird that was said to pierce its own breast to feed its young.

---

who bears the shield, in other words to the left of the beholder).

In the full coat of arms, the central shield is usually flanked by two animals used as supporters, which frequently face inward: that is, one faces *dexter* and the other *sinister* (to the beholder's right, the bearer's left). The animal supporters add another layer of symbolism to the whole heraldic device: for example, the supporters of the arms of the United Kingdom, which were originally devised in 1603, are a lion (the emblem of England) and a unicorn (the emblem of Scotland). These creatures, like the countries they represented, were traditional adversaries, but when shown together they could be used politically to symbolize harmony and the union of opposites.

The shield on the coat of arms bears a helmet adorned with an elaborate crest which commonly includes some heraldic beast. The animal is depicted either in whole or in part (such as just the head, the top half of the body or a single foot or paw).

Heraldic devices include quite simple badges, such as the three fishes (a symbol of the Holy Trinity) in this painting of a jousting knight from 1448. The term "coat of arms" derives from the linen or silk surcoat worn over the armour.

Animals in Context

The ancient Greek philosopher Aristotle's ten-volume *History of Animals* contained some 500 species and ushered in the age of scientific observation. He wrote: "Nature affords indescribable delights to him who is able to see causes, and has the mind of a true investigator. There is something wonderful in every creature of nature. One should not approach the examination of any living being with a long face, but in the certitude that every one of them contains something natural and beautiful."

The flight of the bird, the speed of the deer and the power of the lion must have seemed magical to early humans. Filtered through the human mind, such attributes were interpreted culturally and were used to conjure up analogous images of the human condition. The bird's ability to fly makes it a natural symbol of the flight of the human soul, but sometimes the connection is less obvious. How did the bear come to represent creation? Why does the snake represent rebirth?

The behaviour of each animal contains the seed of the beliefs that grow around it. Different cultures may seize on different attributes to construct very different mythologies, but all cultures, at all times, have woven a close observation of the animal kingdom into their stories and their symbols.

A detail from the Gundestrup Cauldron, showing Cernunnos, the Celtic god of the hunt, with a retinue of game animals. The cauldron, found in a Danish bog, was probably made between the 4th and 3rd century BC in Gaul.

Ape and monkey

Monkeys are found in the Old and the New Worlds. Apes, however, are an exclusively Old World group: gorillas and chimpanzees from Africa, orangutans and gibbons from Asia. Humans have their closest atavistic bond with African apes, having split from them in evolutionary terms between five and ten million years ago. However, for symbolic purposes humans regard all other primates – monkeys and apes – as similar. Their anthropoid appearance, together with their mannerisms, dexterity and mimicry, have qualified them to be seen as mirroring all the vices and virtues of human behaviour.

For many cultures primates represent inquisitiveness, greed and the baser instincts of human nature. The ancient Greek historian Diodorus describes

HANUMAN

In India, the monkey as it appears in Buddhism is both greedy and untrustworthy, although it is a sacred and inviolable animal to the Hindus. It is revered in the god Hanuman, the divine king of monkeys, who is represented as half-human half-monkey, and is the courageous and loyal helper of Rama, the 7th avatar of Vishnu. Endowed with magical powers, this son of the wind god can change his shape, fly through the air and move mountains. Hanuman symbolizes strength and cunning, bestows longevity and has the ability to transform powerful emotions into spiritual energy. He helped Rama to retrieve his wife Sita from the evil Sri Lankan king Ravana.

This 18th-century Tantric illustration is unusual in that it depicts Hanuman in a fearsome aspect, rather than as the devoted helpmate of Rama.

"dog-headed apes [baboons]" as "carrying the womb outside their body". He was referring to the pronounced, inflamed-looking monthly swelling when the female is on heat. Other apes have similar genital displays. In Christian Europe the ape's uninhibited sexuality was an object of disgust well into the 20th century.

The natural curiosity of the monkey has often been interpreted as cunning, avarice and duplicity. In Greece the Cercopes were originally men but Hercules turned them into monkeys in punishment for their trickery. More positive beliefs surround the monkey's obvious intelligence and manual dexterity. In ancient Egypt the baboon god Thoth was credited with the invention of writing, numbers and time itself.

Chimpanzees, like humans, can use their intelligence to develop tools that solve practical problems, such as winkling edible insects out of cracks. Their distant relative the aye-aye has a specially elongated finger which evolved for this purpose, an adaptation chimpanzees emulate by moistening the end of a twig with their sticky saliva and using that to trap their prey.

King Kong embodies the myth that gorillas are incarnations of the most aggressive side of human nature. However, among the traditional societies of Zaire, gorillas were counted as friends of humans, showing them which fruits were good to eat. Gorillas are gentle and dexterous, able to fold nettle leaves so that they may eat them without being stung.

To the Maya of Mexico the monkey, depicted here on the side of a bowl from the late Classical period, was the creator of art, hieroglyphic writing and mathematics.

Lion

Throughout the ancient world the image of the lion was connected with potency and rulership. It was so respected in Assyria that lion hunting was reserved as a royal sport, and in modern Africa the lion is still a figure of chieftainship: Mari-Jata, who founded the Mali empire, was "the Lion of Mali".

Samson is shown overcoming the lion in this 12th-century Austrian altarpiece.

Christianity adopted the imagery of the lion, turning it into the "Lion of Judah", a symbol of Christ. Even the Buddha was occasion-ally depicted on a lion in order to signify his spiritual zeal and enlightened sovereignty. Yet wild lions rarely justify their image of regal courage. In Kenya's Masai Mara game reserve, it was discovered that some 70 per cent of supposed lion kills are actually committed nocturnally by hyenas, which are then driven off by prides of scavenging lions. The only truly regal characteristic of lions is their laziness: they sleep up to 18 hours a day.

THE LION IN EGYPT

The symbolic nature of the lion, like that of many cats, is ambivalent. In Egypt it represented not only the living power of the sun in its identification with the solar deity Ra, but also death and the afterlife, because of its association with Osiris, ruler of the underworld. The lion was also believed to guard the spirit realm. Widely appropriated as a guardian figure and linked with female deities as a symbol of fierce and protective maternity, the lion was sometimes personified as the lion-headed Egyptian goddess Sekhmet, who traditionally guarded against disease and disaster.

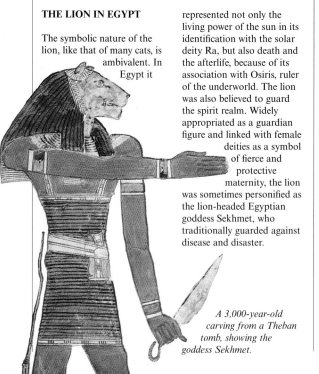

A 3,000-year-old carving from a Theban tomb, showing the goddess Sekhmet.

The lion's roar showed the "jaws of Hell", according to early Christian thought, but it later became a symbol of divine protection, and is now a near-universal image of might. Despite the male's fearsome appearance, it is the female that does most of the hunting. Nevertheless, there is a strict hierarchy at the kill: the dominant male and older females eat first – and get the delicacies such as the liver and genitals – followed by younger females, juveniles and cubs.

In Greek mythology the lion represented the ravening power of death, which Hercules was able to defeat by overcoming the terrifying Nemean lion. He adopted the beast's skin as the emblem of victory. The lion's mythical bravery, and its strength, made it a guardian of the underworld in Egyptian and Greek mythology. It was sometimes depicted on Greek funerary monuments to those who had died on the field of battle. It protected the souls of the dead by frightening away evil spirits, and guarded the living by keeping the shades of the deceased within their tomb. On ancient Sumerian shrines the lion offered protection, not as a creature of the underworld, but as a representative of Nergal, the god of war.

BELOW *In Hindu belief the lion is guardian of the north, and a fearsome attribute of the goddess Durga, the destroyer of evil. In this popular Hindu print she is shown battling a demon in buffalo form, who had dared to attack her and had then attempted to escape her fury by taking on the shape of other animals.*

ABOVE *The winged lion, representing the Saviour's majesty and shown in a 6th-century Italian mosaic, was the emblem of St Mark. In medieval bestiaries, the lion is a favourite subject of Christian moralizing. In an echo of Christ's resurrection, male lions supposedly breathed life into stillborn cubs after three days.*

Tiger

Tigers are the largest of the great cats. They are solitary animals, living alone in well-defined, often thickly-wooded territories until it is time to breed. This has made them more mysterious to humans than lions, and less associated with leadership and royalty.

The tiger gained an imagery of supernatural power in ancient times and, as a sacred mount of Asian warrior gods, evoked respect and power. The Hindu goddess Durga, the "inaccessible one", rides into battle astride a tiger. She is a figure of wrath and destruction, and her mount roars threats at her enemies.

Throughout northeast and southeast Asia the tiger is identified with the ambivalent but masterful spirits of shamanism, traces of which survive in many of the area's religions. In Siberia the tiger-spirit could be invoked by the Tungus shaman, but was also a dangerous soul prowling the forests in search of spiritual prey. Among the Batek Negritos of Malaysia, tigers were believed to infest the central pillar of the world, the dwelling place of Raja Yah, the mystical king of tigers. Batek shamans could shape-shift into tigers in order to become warriors and protect Batek society.

The ruthlessly swift tiger is often seen as a figure of both judgment and punishment. In Thailand, as recently as the late 19th century, if several people were accused of the same serious crime they were all thrown to a tiger. The person who was killed by the cat was guilty. In China the crescent shape of the new moon is envisaged as a tiger's jaws chasing the whole of humanity.

In China, as with the lion in ancient Egypt and Greece, the tiger is identified as the protector of souls and guardian of graves. This bronze ceremonial vessel in the form of a tiger shielding a man in its mouth was made during the Shang period, more than 3,000 years ago.

After the fall of the Roman Empire, tigers were quickly forgotten in Europe. In 1260, Marco Polo described the "striped hunting lions" of Kublai Khan, which were "bigger than ordinary lions", and "skilful at catching game through their great speed".

MAN-EATERS

The reputation of tigers as man-eaters is a recurring motif in India, particularly in 19th-century accounts of life during British rule. However, while tigers can occasionally develop a taste for human flesh, most of them will prey on people only if game is in short supply.

"Tipu's Tiger", a colourful carved-wood effigy of a tiger mauling an English soldier, was commissioned by an Indian potentate to celebrate a victory over the British. The object is in fact an elaborate music box, which plays the sounds of the tiger's triumphant roar as well as the screams of its victim.

Today, while man-eating is not unknown, it is the tigers themselves that are under threat in India. Almost entirely confined to game reserves, their numbers are fast decreasing.

Tipu's tiger.

In this 19th-century Japanese painting by Kuniyoshi Utagawa, one of the "24 Paragons of Filial Piety" confronts a tiger. The 14-year-old Yoko, known in China as Yang Hiang, saved his father from a tiger but died in the act and is commemorated for his virtue and devotion.

Jaguar

When Cortés saw the zoo of Moctezuma the Aztec Emperor in 1517, it contained "lions, tigers and leopards". The "lions" were really pumas and the "leopards" were jaguars, but there are no longer any big cats in the Americas that resemble tigers. By virtue of its size and hunting skills the jaguar is widely known as the "Lord of Animals", the master of spirits. In the mountains and beyond the jungles, the puma is the dominant species, and was more important to the Incas, who imagined their nation as a puma bestriding the Andes. Even here, however, the jaguar was regarded as the father of all cats, partly because pumas are born with spotted pelts, which they lose as they grow older.

Jaguars, unlike many cats, take readily to water both to hunt and play. The ancient Olmecs, who ruled the Gulf of Mexico some 3,000 years ago, owed much of their success to a mastery of irrigation and water control that allowed them to tame their swampy, estuarine environment, which was also the favoured habitat of the jaguar. Since then, the jaguar has been associated with fertility and rainfall.

The Olmec also created the image of the were-jaguar. Even today, in South American hunting and gathering societies the jaguar is the spirit ally of shamans who, in nocturnal ceremonies, consume hallucinogens such as *viho* snuff to aid their transformation into the big cat. They roam the jungle in this supernatural animal form, either bringing illness, death and misfortune or warding them off, according to local beliefs. Some shamans become real jaguars after they die.

The jaguar's name, pelt, claws and fangs are marks of social status, and chiefs will incorporate such elements into their ritual paraphernalia. Jaguar imagery was a central feature of art and belief in many of pre-Columbian America's greatest civilizations. Among the Maya and Aztec, in particular, it stood for royalty and noble lineage.

For the peoples of Central and South America the jaguar's habits – it swims well and is an excellent climber – make it a master of all the elements. The gleam of its eyes, catching the light of night fires in the jungle, meant that when flashlights were first introduced to one Amazonian tribe they were called "jaguar's eyes". Yet the jaguar hunts in daylight as well as nocturnally, and is also associated with the sun. Because it is believed to rear its young in caves, the jaguar represents life, death and the underworld.

JAGUAR MEDICINE

Wherever there is a culture with a tradition of shamanic belief, healers contact powerful medicine spirits to help cure their patients. In South America they often invoke the jaguar. The curing sessions can rely on the animal's reputation as a fierce and predatory hunter, able to frighten away or destroy the evil shades which cause illness and disease. The Heta of South America would rub burnt jaguar skin into a snake-bite, or might try to cure other sicknesses by scratching the victim with a jaguar claw until he or she started to bleed. Jaguar imagery not only cures individuals but also protects against spirits who disrupt the health of society.

Calling on the jaguar spirit, this Heta shaman cures a patient who sits on one jaguar pelt, while a second is passed over his body.

The Matses people of northwestern Peru believe that if they look like a jaguar they will embody its strength and its hunting skills. Almost all adult Matses are decorated with tattoos that cut across their faces in imitation of a big cat's grin. The men wear palm splinters embedded in their upper lips, to represent the jaguar's whiskers, while the women wear similar splinters through their noses.

In the Aztec civilization of Mexico the jaguar was called the ocelotl, *and its courage and fierceness were personified in the elite warrior society known as the "Jaguar Knights", who played a role in the ritual confrontations that preceded human sacrifice. A page from the Codex Zouche, a Mexican painted book (left), shows the warrior King Eight Deer Jaguar Claw capturing an enemy called Four Winds.*
In the mountains of southern Mexico, it is still believed that the jaguar controls the fertilizing rains. It will only send them if blood is shed in its honour, so young men dress themselves in jaguar costumes and engage in bouts of fist-fighting.

Leopard

The leopard is found in both Africa and Asia, and as a result its legends are dispersed across a greater area of the globe than those of any other big cat. The leopard's beautiful pelt has been seen as a "coat of eyes", signifying the watchfulness of the beast, both in the physical and spiritual realms. The leopard embodies courage and aggression, but as a solitary, nocturnal hunter which relies on ambush it has also come to represent cunning. Uniquely among big cats, the leopard stores its kill in a "larder" in the branches of a tree, away from scavengers and other predators. As a consequence, its imagery pervades beliefs about death, the afterlife and the wanderings of the human soul.

The leopard has always had a remarkable reputation for miscegenation. The Romans regarded the animal as an adulterous offspring of the lion and the cheetah (sometimes called a pardel, or a panther), and southern African tradition still holds that the leopard interbreeds with hyenas.

In Africa it is widely believed that witches send out malign souls to do mischief in the form of a leopard. Terrorist "leopard societies" in the 20th century have capitalized on the fear the creature inspires by attacking people with claw-shaped iron prongs in imitation of its savage forays. Members of these societies believed that, by eating the leopard's heart, they would take on its fierceness and bravery.

Sources in the Old Testament define the leopard as the Antichrist, the Beast of the Apocalypse. Hinduism also contains a symbolism of leopard aggression: the god Shiva wears the skin of a leopard which jealous sages had sent to destroy him. The theme is repeated in China, where the leopard is an emblem of warlike behaviour.

In ancient Greece the leopard was the sacred animal of Dionysus, god of wine and presider over orgiastic excess. The cult of Dionysus spread to Europe from the leopard-infested lands of Asia Minor. The god was supposed to have worn a leopard's magical skin during his mythological wanderings in the East, and is often shown riding the beast, as in this mosaic from the House of Masks on Delos, which dates from approximately AD180.

This scene from Tutankhamun's tomb, built between 1347 and 1338BC in the Valley of the Kings in western Thebes, combines the symbolism of the leopard, death and the afterlife. It depicts Tutankhamun's successor, Ay, wearing the magical leopard skin of the priests of Osiris. Ay is engaged in the ritual of opening Tutankhamun's mouth, which would ensure the passage of the dead king's soul to the other world.

RAIN SPIRITS

The leopard's dust-coloured coat, splattered with darker markings like droplets, has linked it in many cultures to water and rainfall. In western Africa it is seen as the storm god, its growl announcing the coming thunder and rain. For the Nuer of southern Sudan, leopard symbolism combines the imagery of rain with that of the land's fertility.

The leopard-skin costume of a Nuer priest is worn as a mark of his people's attachment to the soil.

Cat

Cats found their form very early in the evolution of mammals: the cat family can be traced back to fossils some 40 million years old, and the early cats were already similar to modern species when the ancestors of most mammals were unrecognizable. This is because the cat is a perfectly designed, adaptable killing machine –

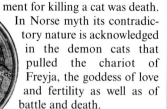

Three cats taken from a 13th-century bestiary

having evolved, it had no need to evolve further. Lithe and silent, the cat comes and goes of its own accord, its natural hunting instincts often emerging suddenly and unexpectedly from a veneer of domestication. Its contradictory nature, in which an appreciation of human affection is combined with a strong independence, fascinates us and inspires a wary admiration.

Ever since its first mention in Egyptian texts around 1500BC, the domestic cat has been an ambivalent symbol of both death and fertility, ill and good omen. The Egyptian cult of the cat was so strong that the punishment for killing a cat was death.

In Norse myth its contradictory nature is acknowledged in the demon cats that pulled the chariot of Freyja, the goddess of love and fertility as well as of battle and death.

In ancient Greece, wild cats were associated with the devotees of Dionysus – the *maenads* or mad women – who wore the animal's skins during their frenzies. Cats are seen as evil shape-shifters in China, and a curse was placed on the cat for not having wept at the death of the Buddha.

Early Christians made the cat a symbol of fertility, but with the spread of the faith through the Roman Empire, pagan deities, such as the goddess of liberty whose cat represented lack of restraint, were branded as demons. Cats became the spawn of Satan, and the "familiars" of witches. Such a view only began to fade in the mid 18th century, paving the way for the cat's current popularity as a domestic pet.

Siamese cats were traditional guardians of temples and palaces. The modern pedigree Siamese has lost the crossed eyes and kinked tail that are still common in its native Thailand. The cat was said to have these features because it concentrated so hard on the objects it was guarding, and wrapped its tail around them for protection.

ABOVE *This 12th-century BC Egyptian drawing depicts a fable in which a cat with a shepherd's crook guards six geese and a nest of eggs.*
LEFT *The ancient Egyptians worshipped the cat-headed goddess Bastet. A living cat personified the deity, and when it died its owner mourned publicly by shaving his eyebrows and mummifying the cat's body.*

THE WITCH'S CAT

In medieval Europe, witches were believed to ride cats to their sabbats, and to suckle them with a third nipple. Black cats especially were supposed to be willing helpers of witches, and used their supernatural knowledge to participate in nightly ceremonies that conjured up the Evil One. The light-reflective eyes of the cat, which are an adaptation to aid its night vision, were interpreted as the flaming eyes of the Devil.

So pervasive were the beliefs among Protestants during the 17th-century witch-craze years that thousands of cats were burned alive inside wooden effigies of the Pope, adding the annihilation of a demon spirit to the symbolic destruction of Catholicism.

This 17th-century woodcut shows the paraphernalia of witchcraft and the Black Sabbath, and the role that cats were supposed to take in the demonic proceedings.

Wolf

The wolf is a powerful and dangerous animal, but it lacks the sharp claws and neckbreaking jaws of the big cats. It is able to kill animals several times its own size only because of its powers of cooperation. Wolves live in packs, structured like tribes with leaders and subordinates. They drive their prey over long distances, making concerted attacks to confuse and exhaust it. Perhaps because of the competition the wolf presented to early humans – who lived and hunted in much the same way – many cultures regarded it as an embodiment of evil.

The image of the wolf as a rapacious predator made it useful to shamans in primitive hunting societies. Lapp shamans could "become" wolves, Tungus shamans are possessed by a wolf spirit, and the myths of other shamanistic cultures tell of sorcerers receiving their calling from a woman disguised as a wolf.

The alert and opportunistic wolf would frequently haunt the fringe of battles, to scavenge corpses and attack the weak and wounded. In Norse mythology the warrior maidens, or Valkyries, ride wolves across the sky, and the cosmic wolf Fenrir, monstrous son of the god Loki, devours Odin at Ragnorak, the battle that destroys the world. The celestial wolf of Celtic myth swallowed the sun each evening to bring on the night.

The wolf is now rare, but it has retained its primeval fascination from times when it was a real threat to everyday life in Europe and North America. It has become a near-universal symbol of predation. The story of Red Riding Hood refers not only to ancestral fears of the animal, but also to predatory males who seduce unsuspecting young women (the colour of the girl's hood suggests that she has just started menstruating). The wolf was a natural peril to Christianity's central symbol, the lamb, and the Christian view that the beast symbolized cruelty and craftiness led to the branding of false prophets as ravening wolves. American Plains Indians regard the prairie wolf or coyote as a trickster, and "a wolf in sheep's clothing" is still a figure of deceit.

Along the northwest coast of America the wolf is a powerful spirit-animal which endows the shaman with supernatural abilities and, being "strong medicine", helps cure his patients. A wolf mask would enable the shaman to contact the fierce spirits of the hunt, and the hat (above) of a fully-fledged Tlingit shaman is protectively decorated with wolf emblems. The uninitiated were in danger, however: the ceremonial Tlingit club (right), made of wood, shell, hair and teeth, shows a novice being carried off by a wolf.

ROMULUS AND REMUS

One account of the founding of Rome occurs in the story of Romulus and Remus. Illicit sons of the war god Mars and a seduced Vestal Virgin, the twins were set adrift on the Tiber to die but washed up outside the cave of Lupercal where a great she-wolf discovered them and nurtured them. When Romulus and Remus subsequently founded the city of Rome, their lupine foster mother became not only its symbol, but also an expression of valour and the predatory nature of the Roman empire. Lupercalia, the Roman festival of a fertility god associated with Pan, honoured the wolf's role in legend.

A bronze statue of the she-wolf suckling the twins from the Capitoline Museum in Rome.

The wolf's howling is a way of bonding it to its pack. Other bonding behaviour can be mistaken by humans for displays of affection. The dog that licks its owner's face is replicating the actions of wolves which lick each other's muzzles to prompt food regurgitation, for sharing. Such mistaken cues help explain why early humans formed close ties to animals they hated and feared.

Dog

No animals are more familiar to us than dogs or more often loved and trusted. This physical and emotional relationship seems to grow more important as urban societies lose touch with the instinctual world which even the most domesticated dog still inhabits. The emotional therapy of living with a dog is not a discovery of modern psychology but something people have known about for thousands of years.

In the ancient world, where death was ever-present, dogs were widely seen as suitable guides and companions not just in life but also in the spirit-world – perhaps because their superior powers of smell and hearing make them aware of things that are beyond the limited scope of human sensory abilities. The Ainu people of Japan, for example, believed that their dogs had the psychic power to detect ghosts. For the Incas, the howling of a dog could foretell the death of a relative.

White dogs were sacrificed by the Iroquois as intercessors with the gods. Dogs were portrayed in ancient Roman funerary art, because their love and fidelity survived beyond the grave. The pre-Columbian Mayan civilization buried dogs with their masters to guide them across the waters of the after-world. A similar belief in the dog as a soul-companion explains the ancient Parsee custom of bringing a dog to a deathbed so that the dying person could look into its eyes. The central Asian practice of feeding bodies to dogs to speed the passage of souls to the afterlife was offensive to some, and may have contributed to the Semitic and Islamic view that dogs were unclean.

As dogs range in real life from amiable friends to aggressive hunters and guardians, so their supernatural counterparts varied also. In mythology, fierce dogs served many underworld deities such as Yama in India or Hades and Hecate in Greece. Dog-headed Lords of Death with more positive roles included Anubis in Egypt and the Aztec Xoltl who guided the sun safely through the underworld into which it sank each night. Dogs also appear in iconography as companions of supreme gods, such as the Vedic Indra, and with other warrior and hunting gods, such as the Celtic goddess Epona. In cultures from Africa and Melanesia to Siberia and America, dogs and related wild species such as coyotes, jackals and dingoes were often heroes – intelligent, resourceful and helpful to mankind.

To prepare a mummified Egyptian for the afterlife, a priest wears the jackal mask of Anubis. This god, sometimes shown instead with a dog's head, was once Lord of the Dead and later master of funerary ceremonies. He led souls to judgment.

This watercolour by William Blake (1757–1827) shows the three-headed dog Cerberus who guarded the entrance to Hades in Greek myth. His duty was not only to prevent the dead from leaving the underworld but also to deny the living access, although both Orpheus and Odysseus outwitted him, and Hercules led him above ground to show off his own strength before returning him to Hades.

The dingo, shown here in an Aboriginal rock painting, is a species of the same genus, Canis, as the tame dog, and resembles the earliest known domesticated dogs in Europe. Aboriginals took such dogs with them thousands of years ago when they migrated to Australia, probably through Melanesia. Even after the dogs ran wild, many lived around Aboriginal camps and some are raised as pets.

WATCHDOGS

Protection of ethical laws – or of the defenceless – is an important strand in the symbolism of the dog. For their aggressive behaviour, the outspoken Greek philosopher Diogenes and his followers were insultingly called Cynics (from the Greek word for dog) – but adopted the name gladly as moral watchdogs. As a Latin pun with similar meaning, the Dominicans were sometimes called "dogs of the Lord" for defending Christian doctrine. In China, the Buddhist Lion Dog or dog of Fo is the guardian of the law.

A "beware of the dog" mosaic, from a 2nd-century AD Roman villa.

Bear

The brown and black bears of northern Asia, Europe and America do not actually hibernate. After gorging on fruit, berries and nuts in the autumn to put on a thick layer of fat, they merely sleep lightly through the winter. Their body temperature drops by only a few degrees, and they are able to rouse

An Arabic illustration of the Great Bear.

themselves quickly if disturbed, whereas true hibernators, such as marmots, become rigid as their temperature falls close to zero. The bear cannot afford true hibernation, because it gives birth and suckles its young in the winter while "buried" in the ground. It emerges in spring with its cubs, which has led to its being seen as the embodiment of rebirth, wisdom and fertility.

Classical antiquity preserved the primitive belief that bear cubs are born without form, and that their mothers "lick them into shape", so creating order out of chaos. The bear is thus widely seen as a symbol of creation. In Greek mythology it was the sacred animal of Artemis the huntress who, although a virgin, was also the goddess of childbirth. Both the ancient Greeks and Hindus identified the Ursa Major (Great Bear) constellation as a bear,

and in Hindu lore the constellation was regarded as the source of all universal energy, responsible for the succession of the seasons.

The warriors and chiefs of Teutonic mythology had bears as guardian spirits, and among the Norse the feared berserkers went into battle dressed only in bear-skins, yet apparently remained unharmed by sword or fire. Such imagery led the Christians of the Dark Ages to regard the bear as a cruel and vicious animal, an image of carnality and the devil.

The bear remains a powerful symbol among more recent hunting societies. According to the Inuit the "Mother of Bears" gives shamans the ability to see into the spirit world. Both Inuit and Lapp shamans may shape-shift into bears for their spirit journeys.

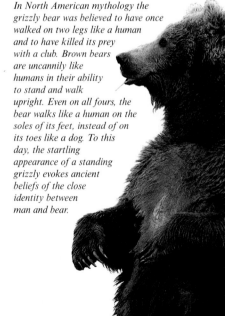

In North American mythology the grizzly bear was believed to have once walked on two legs like a human and to have killed its prey with a club. Brown bears are uncannily like humans in their ability to stand and walk upright. Even on all fours, the bear walks like a human on the soles of its feet, instead of on its toes like a dog. To this day, the startling appearance of a standing grizzly evokes ancient beliefs of the close identity between man and bear.

Among shamanic peoples, an animal spirit often chooses its shaman, rather than the other way round. On the northwest coast of America the bear is one of the most eagerly sought after guardian spirits, granting physical strength and the ability to perform feats of daring. Its image is often carved in totem poles. As a mythical ancestor it is regarded as particularly sacred. Here the image of a bear has been woven into the blanket of a chief of the Tlingit tribe.

THE BEAR AS SPIRIT GUIDE

Shamanism has long embraced the bear as a kindred spirit, symbol of rebirth and possessor of magical wisdom and powers of healing. Among the Native American Blackfoot, the bear shaman (right) makes powerful medicine during the bear dance in which he dons the animal's skin and imitates its grunting and movements. Carrying his mystical spear and dangling the bear's power-laden claws from his arms, the shaman growls like the grizzly and sings to the good and evil spirits. In imitation of the way in which the bear treats its prey, the shaman rolls his patient around and paws at him in order to frighten the illness away.

Polar bear

The most impressive predator of the polar regions, the white bear of the north offers an inspiring image to the Inuit people. In this harsh landscape, where the struggle for life is intense, the polar bear embodies vital qualities. A successful hunter of seals, it is strong, patient, seemingly wise, remarkably cunning. The Inuit claim that they have learned from the bear how to kill a sleeping walrus with a block of ice or stone, how to wait persistently by an ice hole for a seal or fish to appear, how to build iglus of ice and snow. The iglu and the polar bear's maternity den have several features in common: the low entrance tunnel, the ramp leading to a raised chamber, the ventilation hole. Sharing the same territory and prey, Inuit and bears lead their lives in a close and suggestive parallel.

Among the Labrador Inuit the polar bear was seen as a form of Tuurngasuk, the Great Spirit. He appears as a giant polar bear to "devour" the aspiring shaman prior to his ritual rebirth. Alaskans tell stories about a ten-legged bear, Kokogiak, said to lure hunters by waving its front legs in the air, howling "ko-ko-ko" as if calling for help.

The Dorset culture, which flourished in the Arctic $c.500$BC–$c.$AD1000, left "flying" bear carvings on ivory, which may depict shamanic spirit journeys: the polar bear accompanying the shaman on his otherworldly flight. The posture of the bears on these ancient artefacts, as well as on more recent carvings, in fact accurately depicts a polar bear swimming. Thus, the spiritual resonance of the bear may owe a debt to close observation of nature.

In icy water, polar bears depend on a layer of blubber for insulation. On land, they benefit from dense wool, as well as hollow guard hairs which channel short-wave energy from the sun to the bear's black skin. The subtle pale, sometimes yellowish tones seen in polar bears in the wild are caused by refraction of sunlight in the colourless guard hairs. Bears captive in zoos sometimes look greenish – the effect of freshwater algae colonizing broken guard hairs.

INUIT INITIATION

The closeness of the relationship between human and bear in Inuit belief is shown by the animal's prominence in the initiation rites of young boys. To be a man is to be a successful hunter, and the qualities that are needed to achieve this status have to be gained from the spirit of the polar bear. The ultimate test of manhood is the killing of this most feared and respected of adversaries. Because of the creature's sacredness, its killing and dismemberment are surrounded by ritual precautions. The boy's father sings songs to the bear's spirit to ensure that his son will always be a successful hunter.

A small (3 inch/8cm) carving of two polar bears wrestling, from the northwest American coast, 19th century.

A modern Inuit painting of a polar bear and cub. The pale coat of the polar bear, contrasting with the dark icy sea, is linked to the imagery of the moon. The Moon-Man, patron of hunters, was said to be clad in the skin of a bear.

ABOVE *A 16th-century illustration of William Barents' last voyage to the Arctic, showing crew members hunting bear with harpoons.*
Pioneering visitors to the region found the polar bear terrifying. It raided camps, and could not easily be scared by gunfire – perhaps because it was used to the crack of sea ice. Killing polar bears became a form of entertainment bred of nervous insecurity. Cubs were killed or shipped off to zoos. The European attitude contrasts sharply with the Inuits' respect for their quarry.

Elephant

African elephants are the largest surviving land animals. They grow throughout life, so that the oldest specimens are likely to be the biggest, and may stand 13 feet (4m) tall at the shoulder. Asian elephants are slightly smaller, but still imposing: they are decorated in gold cloth and jewels for important ceremonies in India, Sri Lanka, Malaysia, Indonesia and Thailand. The supreme Vedic deity Indra chose an elephant as his mount for cosmic journeys.

Aristotle called the elephant "The beast that passeth all others in wit and mind", and its memory and intelligence have been noted ever since it was first domesticated in the Indus Valley, around 5500BC. The people of Thailand whisper secrets into an elephant's ear and ask for solutions to their problems.

Early humans were familiar with many more species of elephant than the two that survive today. Siberians dug traps for woolly mammoths, pygmy elephants roamed the Mediterranean, and one Mayan pillar depicts people riding mastodons in South America. Folk memories of elephants have survived where the animals have not. Among the Tuareg of the Sahara, where it is extinct, the elephant is seen as a benefactor. To the ancient Greeks the elephant was especially wise, and even its breath could cure illness.

A belief in the wise nature of the elephant is nurtured by its great gentleness despite its size and strength. If one member of a herd is harmed, the rest will come to its aid even at considerable risk to themselves. Elephants care for their injured by using their delicate, versatile trunks to apply styptic clay to wounds, in order to staunch the flow of blood.

A 19th-century painting of Indra, riding his elephant, Airavata.

ELEPHANT GRAVEYARD

It was the Roman writer Pliny who first claimed that elephants bury their dead. He wrote that when an elephant dies, other members of the herd caress its body with their trunks, covering it with earth and branches. Later they remove the tusks and scatter them in the countryside. His account is based on the way that elephants gather to comfort a dying herd member. The absence of tusks from elephant corpses, however, is usually because they have been stolen by humans.

There is no evidence for an elephants' graveyard, where old tuskers go to die. The occasional large collection of bones may mark the site of a mass slaughter by poachers, or the location of the last water-hole in a drought, where a herd congregated and starved to death.

An 18th-century Indian carving of Ganesha. In Hindu belief Ganesha is the elephant-headed son of Shiva and Parvati. Regarded as the god of sagacity, he is worshipped as the lord of the demigods who attend Shiva, and he is frequently invoked at the beginning of a task since he is believed to remove obstacles. Ganesha is widely revered as the patron of business people.

BELOW *Elephants have long been threatened by hunters seeking their ivory tusks. The ancient Greeks regarded elephant ivory as having a lustre akin to human flesh, and used it alongside gold in their most sacred statues.*

Horse

Early man hunted horses for food, and it was not until 2000BC that the Eurasian wild horse, the ancestor of all domestic horses, was tamed by the nomads of the steppes. At first the horse was only used to draw loads, because of its natural tendency to buck predators – or riders – off its back. Over the centuries, horses were increasingly broken for riding, but it was only when the Chinese invented the stirrup in the 5th century AD that cavalry became a popular means of warfare. Although the earliest of the domesticated horses had drawn war-chariots, they were clearly servants of the charioteers. Now, for the first time, man and horse were seen as partners in the work of death and destruction – as shown in 13th-century accounts of the Mongol hordes.

To a Mongolian shaman the horse was also a *psychopomp*, or imaginary mount, which he rode on celestial jour- neys and which carried the spirits of the dead into the other world. Christian teaching has also regarded the horse as representing the swift passage of life, and in the vision of St John the four horsemen of the Apocalypse – death, war, pestilence and famine – mark the last days of mankind.

In Celtic Britain and Gaul the horse goddess Epona was associated with water, fertility and death. There was widespread sacrifice of horses in Celtic Europe in the belief that they would become soul-mounts for their masters' symbolic ride of death.

Yet, alongside their historic role as war machines, horses have always been valued companions and workers, tradi-tionally connected with life, intelligence and divination. Hinduism associates the horse with Vishnu's last appearance on earth, during which he brings peace and salvation.

Startlingly realistic representations of wild horses executed on the walls of caves, such as this image which was painted at Lascaux in France some 15,000 years ago, are the earliest expressions of humankind's interest in the horse. Antler and ivory carvings dating from the same period show horses wearing what may be halters, suggesting that at this early time the animal may have been kept even if not ridden.

According to Norse mythology, horses could understand the will of the gods. Odin himself rode an immensely strong, eight-legged grey stallion, called Sleipnir. This magical steed was an offspring of the trickster figure Loki, and helped to build a wall around Asgard, the home of the gods.

CHIVALRY

As a symbol of supremacy, generosity and courage, the horse was a suitable expression of medieval chivalry – the very word derives from the Latin and French roots for "horse". Combining the notion of romantic love, the imagery of heraldic beasts and the role of the knight as bastion against the forces of heathenism, the horse carried its master into battles for king, country and faith (as shown in the 14th-century English tapestry, right). So strong was the emotive link between knights and their mounts that massed cavalry was employed in warfare – often, as at Balaclava in the Crimean War, with disastrous results – long after it had been made redundant. Polish cavalry even charged German tanks during the Second World War.

Swine

Tusked wild boars, which can weigh 500lb (240kg) and stand nearly 4 feet (1.3m) high at the shoulder, were among the most dangerous animals ever hunted with simple weapons. They were feared for their speed and aggression and respected for their fighting courage throughout ancient Europe, North Africa, India and Asia. As a result, their symbolism could range from

This ceremonial boar's head mask from Bali is made of painted wood adorned with bristles.

forceful rulership to destructive tyranny. Their long (and continuing) history as prized trophies of the chase explains their importance in many countries as virility emblems of warriors or warrior gods – and as sacrificial offerings. In northern Europe, boar meat was eaten ritually and sometimes buried with men killed in battle. The boar's head was a special delicacy for gods and heroes.

The boar was seen as a primordial force of nature. The Greek myth of the beautiful Adonis, gored to death by a boar, is a coded story encapsulating the wisdom that death is necessary to new life. Adonis, who was a grain or vegetation god, was worshipped in the form of a boar, so in the myth he is the agent of his own death. Resurrection rites of Adonis invoked and celebrated the spring rebirth of nature. In a Norse myth that similarly celebrates the continuity of nature, the monster boar Saerhrimnir was continually reborn to be hunted and eaten by the immortal heroes of Valhalla.

Celtic peoples, who told similar stories of miraculously self-renewing herds of swine, regarded the boar as a sacred and prophetic beast with magical protective qualities. Just as Nordic warriors sought to borrow the power of boars by wearing tusked helmets, druids called themselves "boars" to identify themselves with the animal's knowledge of the forest and its secrets.

Sows were also symbols of fertility, as in Egyptian imagery of the sky goddess Nut suckling her many piglets (the stars). As they exemplified bountiful mother goddesses, pigs were widely sacrificed in the hope of ensuring good harvests. Although the folklore of pigs is usually affectionate, they were greedy, unclean scavengers in Jewish, Islamic and Christian traditions, in part perhaps because they are very difficult to herd, and are therefore anathema to nomadic peoples.

Depictions of the Buddhist wheel of existence show the pig (ignorance) as one of the three animals binding mankind to sensual desires. Although pigs are certainly hearty eaters, the link with ignorance seems based on nothing more than the pig's habit of keeping its head low to the ground.

THE CELTIC BOAR

Celtic reverence for boars did not prevent their being hunted with spear and horse – a sport called "pig-sticking" in India, where it continues (although with less ritual significance). The tables were turned by the boar in the Irish tale of Diarmaid and Gráinne. The story tells of the maiden Gráinne who was unwillingly betrothed to the cultural hero Finn. She eloped with Diarmaid, but they were confronted by Diarmaid's foster brother, the great magic boar of Bean Ghulban. The boar mortally wounded Diarmaid and his only hope was to drink water cupped in Finn's hands. Remembering Gráinne, Finn let the water seep through his fingers and Diarmaid died.

A Celtic cult wagon of bronze, c. 6th century BC, *shows a boar hunt.*

These 12th-century Romanesque ceiling paintings (below right) from a Swiss church at Zillis depict scenes from the story of the Gadarene swine. Jesus drove the devilish spirits out of a possessed man and into a herd of pigs which stampeded over a cliff into the abyss. Christianity saw the pig and the wild boar equally as symbols of brutishness, sensuality and insatiable appetite, and thus as personifications of the devil.

The function of this wooden figure (left) from the Nicobar Islands was to ward off evil spirits with the aid of its fearsome tusks. On the Melanesian island of Malekula the boar's curved white tusks were seen as the crescent moon, and represented the continuance of life after death. The animal's ritual sacrifice was a necessary offering for a successful voyage to the underworld. In other places in southeast Asia, the boar also played a central role in beliefs about the afterlife.

Deer

Swift and elusive, the deer was often represented (especially in the form of a white doe or white stag) as the epitome of the soul, or as a divine messenger. In Celtic myth deer drew the chariot of Flidass, goddess of the chase, and were revered as conveyors of souls to the spirit world. Shamans around Lake Baikal in Siberia daubed their ritual implements with the blood of a newly sacrificed reindeer: the animal's spirit bore them on their soul-journeys.

Deer shed their antlers each year, and grow them only for the rutting season, when the clashing antlers of competing males can be heard for miles, fostering a reputation for virility. The gory appearance of the antlers when their velvet is first shed may have led to the stag possessing a more violent reputation than is justified. Well into the 20th century, Siberian shamans danced in horned reindeer masks, not only to promote success in the hunt but also, by emulating the reindeers' rutting behaviour, to encourage them to breed successfully and provide plentiful herds for the future. This may have played some part in creating the lore of stag-gods such as Cernunnos and in promoting the sacrificial rites surrounding cults such as that of Actaeon. In Greek myth the hunter Actaeon mistakenly stumbled upon Diana, the goddess of the hunt, as she was bathing. As punishment she turned him into a stag and he was chased and killed by his own dogs.

A gentler approach to the animal is contained in Buddhist teachings, where the deer symbolizes meditation and meekness. Deer on either side of the circle of the Wheel of Law signify the Buddha's first sermon, which was preached in the deer park at Sarnath.

Each year, a stag's antlers grow an extra branch, clearly exhibiting its age and growing strength, and in Chinese culture the deer represents longevity and official success. Similarly, in Japan, it is an attribute of the gods of longevity, but here it can also represent solitariness and melancholy.

These prehistoric rock carvings found at Cemmo, Italy, reflect the vital importance of deer to early hunting cultures. The deer was large enough to provide plentiful meat, so that a single kill was enough to keep a family, or even a small tribe, fed. Yet at the same time the deer was a far less dangerous quarry than other large mammals such as buffaloes, elephants or aurochs.

A member of the northern Siberian Evenk people sits surrounded by reindeer antlers. Blood from the antlers of freshly killed reindeer is believed to be rejuvenating.

CERNUNNOS

The Celtic deity Cernunnos, head adorned with antlers, embodied the virility and aggressiveness of all male horned creatures. He is often depicted with a ram-headed serpent in attendance, and may bear phallic or other fertility symbols. The twisted metal torc he holds, or wears about his neck, signifies his divine status.

The Celts equated Cernunnos with Dis Pater, the god of the dead, and with the Wild Hunt during which the hounds of Hell collected

Part of a beaten silver panel from the Gundestrup Cauldron, a Danish cult vessel dating from the 4th or 3rd century BC.

the souls of the dying to take them to the underworld.

Cernunnos was lord of both domestic and wild animals: he is often depicted with deer or horses. Leaves in his antlers also show him to be a god of the forest. Most Celtic deities have merely local significance, but Cernunnos is found throughout Celtic myth.

The metamorphosis of St Nicolas, a stately Russian saint in bishop's robes who rode a white horse, into Father Christmas began in the early 19th century. White-whiskered and dressed in red, Father Christmas travels in a sleigh drawn by flying reindeer, suggesting a link with the Siberian shamanic use of white-spotted scarlet hallucinogenic toadstools which transformed the shamans into reindeer spirits.

Bison and buffalo

Members of this bovine family are found all around the world from the Indian buffalo in Asia and the Cape buffalo in southern and western Africa to the bison (also known as the buffalo) that once covered the prairies of North America in their millions before their near-annihilation by settlers. *Bison priscus*, over 6 feet (1.8m) tall, was well known to prehistoric humans in Europe who provided the first-known depictions in the painted caves of southwest France and northern Spain. The great physical strength of the creature, and the consequent difficulty of hunting it with primitive weapons, combined with the bountiful yield of its carcass once obtained, would have readily aroused a sense of awe and reverence, and it was regarded as a deity at the centre of a Stone Age cult for several thousand years. It has also been symbolized as a potent creator being in many more recent societies.

For the Zulus of southern Africa, the buffalo can possess the soul of a human. Among African pastoralist societies such as the Bantu, the buffalo is widely revered and is a sacrifice at important sacred ceremonies, a ritual status it also achieves in southeast Asia. In central and northern Asia, black

BUFFALO DANCES

When food was short for the Mandan Indians of North America, the warriors would don buffalo masks and begin a dance which they believed would change the direction of the wandering herds to bring them near their village.

A group of up to 15 men, carrying their bows and arrows and wearing horned masks, performed this sacred dance in front of the Great Medicine lodge. The dance lasted for hours, mimicking the endurance of the buffalo, which in spite of its bulk can run at full speed for 10 or 12 minutes and survive a temperature of 150°F (85°C) on very little water. As one by one the dancers fell out of the dance with fatigue, others replaced them until the buffaloes appeared. After the hunt, the choicest parts of the buffalo were offered to the Great Spirit.

A buffalo dance painted by George Catlin c.1832.

buffaloes are sacrificed to the god of the chase. Occasionally the Buddha appeared in the animal's form. The Vedic god of the dead rode a buffalo, and in another Hindu myth the warrior goddess Durga is portrayed as slaying the great buffalo Mahisha, despite his many transformations to escape her, during her cosmic battle with demons.

Among the Plains Indians of North America, nature and spirit combined to produce the most elaborate buffalo symbolism. The buffalo was a manifestation of the supreme being for the Oglala Dakota Sioux, and played a central role in the vision-quest ceremonies of those tribes that practised the sun dance, a ritual of self-torment.

ABOVE *For at least 15,000 years the bison played a central role in the physical and spiritual life of humans. It figures among the earliest graphic reproductions of animals painted on the walls of Paleolithic caves such as Lascaux in France where artists worked in near-darkness, often using the contours of the rock to enhance their work.*

ABOVE *A drawing of a bison herd by a European traveller. The power of the individual animal and the seemingly invincible rush of the immense herds were evocative images for the American Plains dwellers who depended on the bison as a vital resource for its skin, flesh, bones, fat, tendons and horn.*

RIGHT *An 18th-century watercolour of the sage Lao-tzu, a contemporary of Confucius. In Taoist belief Lao-tzu rides a buffalo, which symbolizes his final triumph over man's animal nature. In some Taoist tales, the buffalo is green; in others it gradually changes colour from black to white as it becomes tamed, a metaphor for the spirit overcoming base desires.*

Bull and cow

The domestication of cattle was one of the most significant events in human history. Sheep and goat herders were still largely migratory peoples, seasonally driving their flocks between pastures. The ox allowed humans to till the soil, settle and build villages and towns. The ancestor of domestic cattle, the Oriental aurochs, was so large and ferocious that the Babylonians and Assyrians, who were the first to use oxen, thought it impossible to tame without divine help. Early accounts of the ox (*rimu* in Babylonian, *re-em* in Hebrew) are written in terms of such awe that the classical world, used to dealing with cattle pacified by generations of breeding, imagined that they must refer to some more fabulous beast. The Authorized version of the Book of Job, taken from the Greek, asks, "Canst thou bind the unicorn with his bands in the furrow? Wilt thou trust him, because his strength is great?" Whereas the original Hebrew refers to the *re-em*.

Most bull symbolism refers to the

A fertility festival among the Dinka of Sudan. The young girls who are to be courted carry cows' horns. The men who come courting bring special, pampered oxen, called "song bulls", with them.

animal's strength and fury, and is expressed in rituals of divination and bloody sacrifice. Echoes of such beliefs survive today in modern Spanish bull fights.

Because of its virility the bull has always been associated with the life-creating sun. The ancient Hittites of Anatolia worshipped a sun god whose chariot was harnessed to bulls. The bull's roar presaged rain for the Sumerians, and in Norse mythology the animal was identified with both Thor, the god of thunder, and Freyja, the goddess of fertility. The Hindu god Indra also appears as Agni, the fertilizing bull.

Cows have almost never been sacrificed: they are too docile and too useful. For the Sudanese Dinka they provide life-giving milk, their urine is a cleansing agent, as well as a dye, and their blood can be drunk in small quantities without really hurting the animals. Primitive pastoralists' reverence for their herds survives in Hinduism, where cows are protected as sacred and revered as nourishers of humanity.

At Knossos in Minoan Crete, "bull-leaping" rituals, shown here on a 1500BC fresco from the palace walls, may have inspired the Greek legend of the Minotaur, the bull-headed monster which devoured yearly tributes of 14 young Athenians, until killed by the hero Theseus.

CRESCENT HORNS

In ancient Egypt the sacred cow goddess Hathor (shown on an 11th-century tomb wall from Thebes) was the protector of women and goddess of joy. She cherished the dead and gave her milk as nourishment to the pharaoh Amenhotep II. Her benign temperament is illustrated by her cosmic role as creator of the world who enclosed the sun in her breast each evening. Like many bovine deities, Hathor was a goddess of the sky, an association that arose in most cultures because the curved horns of bulls and cows were thought to resemble the crescent moon. At Memphis in Egypt, tribute was paid to the Apis bull who was conceived by fertilizing moonlight, and sacred bulls were mummified.

A 2nd-century AD Roman sculpture of the Persian god Mithra, who also became the centre of a cult in the Roman empire. Mithra was usually depicted slaying a great bull, thereby immortalizing man's victory over his animal nature. Initiates into the cult of Mithraism were baptized in the blood of a bull.

A wallpainting from the Tomb
of Nebamun in Thebes,
c.1400 BC, showing an
inspection of cattle. The cult
of cattle ownership spread
from Egypt to most of Africa.

Historically, cattle have
been major contributors to the
desertification of Egypt, and it
has been suggested that the
combined populations of
humans and cattle may now
exceed the carrying capacity
of the land.

Goat and sheep

In the Fertile Crescent of the Middle East, where farming originated, the first domesticated flocks of animals were goats and sheep. Although selective breeding has differentiated them, the two species are not always easy to tell apart in the wild, or in their primitive domesticated forms, which are still found in Asia and the

A 15th-century fresco from Padua, showing the zodiacal sign of Capricorn the ram.

Mediterranean. They are distinguished by the fact that sheep have scent glands on their fore and hind legs, goats on their fore legs only.

The male goat and the ram are widely associated with virility, owing partly to their vigorous coupling and partly to the phallic imagery of their horns. Wild goats, and ancestral sheep such as the argali of the central Asian plateau, can have horns with a curve of more than 5 feet (1.5m). The ram was one of the

first objects of cult worship, as is evident from 10,000-year-old Saharan rock paintings which depict humans worshipping a ram with a solar disk between its horns. In the myths of classical antiquity the shape of the ram's horns stood for masculine potency, while their hollow insides represented the cornucopia, or horn of plenty, and the energy that brought fertility and wealth. However, Jason's quest for the Golden Fleece, which came from a fabulous ram with the power of speech and flight, was a search for spiritual as well as earthly wealth.

Christianity identifies the goat and the ram with lustful sinners and with the devil. Christ, the innocent Lamb of God, can simultaneously be portrayed as the scapegoat, burdened with the sins of humanity.

LEFT *In Egypt the ram, shown on the wall of the tomb of Queen Nefertari (1290–1220BC), was a solar symbol of creative heat and the personification of Amun-Ra, the "mightiest of created beings". Always depicted with wavy horns, Amun-Ra symbolized the daily cycle of solar regeneration, and a sacred ram believed to be the living incarnation of Amun-Ra was kept at Karnak. The symbolic potency of the ram was later adopted by Alexander the Great, who was shown wearing a ram's-horn head-dress on coins which represented him as World Conqueror.*

THE GOAT GOD PAN

A 2,400-year-old silver disk shows the god Pan, from Ercolano, near Naples. Originating in myths of the mountainous region of Arcadia, Pan was born with the hindlegs, horns and beard of a goat. He was a shepherd deity, the protector of flocks, who made goats and ewes fertile. He was also a mischievous dweller in woods and shady groves who delighted in frightening lonely travellers, which is the origin of the word "panic". He amused himself by chasing nymphs, one of whom changed into a reed to escape him. The god consoled himself by cutting reeds to make a musical instrument: the panpipes.

The sheep is the first domestic animal mentioned in the Bible, and the most commonly sacrificed. In the New Testament Christ is the Lamb of God, who is sacrificed for the expiation of all sins. He is shown in this 5th-century Byzantine mosaic as a shepherd.

Rabbit and hare

The human capacity for "sympathetic projection" – seeing real faces and things in abstract patterns, and, moreover, broadly agreeing on what is seen – is nowhere better illustrated than in the legends of the rabbit and the hare. Disparate cultures from across the world have seen one or other of these creatures rendered in the shadows and craters that Western Europeans have tended to call "the man in the moon". Native Americans tell the tale of the Great Hare Manabazho who dwells in the moon. As the ultimate provider of wind and water, he is a culture hero who transforms mankind's animal nature to a higher plane. He represents the Great Spirit Manitou, the creator.

Lunar associations occur also in Buddhism, where the Great Hare was an incarnation of the Buddha who put it in the moon in gratitude for its self-sacrifice by leaping into a fire to roast when he was hungry.

Connections with the moon led to parallels between the hare and menstruation (medieval bestiaries describe the hare as imparting "its melancholy nature" to all those who ate it), and therefore fertility, fruitfulness and love. In this guise, in Graeco-Roman tradition, the animal was an attribute of Aphrodite and a companion of Cupid. Rabbits produce more young than hares, but both are cunning mothers. Each litter is dispersed between several different burrows (in the case of rabbits) or *forms* (shallow depressions used by hares), each of which the mother visits secretly only once each day, for less than five minutes, to nurse her young.

The Romans noted in their campaign against Boudicca, Queen of the Iceni, that the hare was an important animal for the early Britons, and that Boudicca would release one as a good omen before battle.

In later European customs the "Easter bunny" was the bringer of dawn and the creator of life, a folk memory of the Anglo-Saxon moon goddess Eostre who appeared with a hare's head, symbolizing springtime, renewal and the new moon. Celtic moon deities were sometimes depicted holding a hare, and in Celtic lore the hare also appears with gods of the hunt.

Viewing pagan beliefs with distrust and ambiguity, Christianity represented the hare as a symbol of timidity, lust and promiscuity. But in one of its Christian aspects the hare, as a symbol of defencelessness, was identified with those who put their trust in the protective strength of Christ. The white hare at the feet of the Virgin Mary signified moral triumph over the baser instincts.

The role of the hare and rabbit as tricksters occurs most famously in Brer Rabbit, *a 19th-century American rendering of traditional African stories taken to the New World plantations by slaves. This hare mask comes from the Yoruba people of West Africa.*

LONG LIFE

In China the hare represents longevity and reproductive power. Chinese myth portrays the hare as the protector of all wild animals, and in its cosmic form it is the white hare in the moon, which pounds a mixture to create the elixir of immortality. In fact the average age of hares and rabbits in the wild is little more than a year. The oldest known wild hare was not quite 13 years old. While some rabbits and hares have become pests, others are in danger of extinction. The Japanese government has declared the endangered amami rabbit a "living natural monument" in an effort to conserve it.

An 18th-century Chinese silk embroidery of the hare in the moon, from an emperor's robe.

This panel from a painted clay vase from ancient Mexico shows the rabbit in a scene from Mayan myth. The lords of the underworld have been defeated by the Hero Twins – two demigods who, according to the Mayan sacred book, the Popul Vuh, also defeated an early, false sun, and set the stage for the emergence of humanity. The underworld gods, or Xibalba, were stripped of not only their power but also their clothes.

The rabbit, the inventor of writing, is in a position of authority as a scribe in a generally illiterate society, and stands sternly on a stone platform in the form of a Kawac monster. He holds the cape, hat and staff of one of the old defeated gods, who begs to be given back his garments. The Maya were among the peoples who saw a rabbit in the moon, and lunar rabbits occur frequently in the art of pre-Hispanic Mexico.

Male hares chase each other round the fields and engage in "boxing matches" in order to determine superiority during their breeding season. Males and females may also box during their courtship ritual. Although the season lasts from January to August, this boisterous behaviour has given rise to the saying, "mad as a March hare". Such behaviour, as well as the animal's habit of wrongfooting and erratically changing direction when pursued, may also contribute to its reputation as a trickster (see p.45).

Tortoise and turtle

In mythical accounts there is often little difference drawn between the aquatic turtle and the land-bound tortoise (sometimes also known as turtle). The two were not differentiated even by naturalists until the 16th century. Because of the sturdiness of their shells, and the apparent weariness of their movements, both animals are commonly portrayed as carrying the world on their backs among peoples as diverse as the Hindus of Asia and the Huron of America.

Taoist cosmologies, on the other hand, as well as those of the American Sioux, envisaged the universe encompassed by the shell of the turtle. Hindu cosmology conceived the two-part shell as the universe, the flatter, lower half – or plastron – representing the earth, and the upper rounded carapace the celestial sphere. Native Americans of the Prairies recognized the rumble of earthquakes as the cosmic turtle shaking its earthly shell.

A connection between the turtle (which can lay up to 200 eggs in a single clutch) and fertility is found in Hindu belief, where the animal is identified with Prajapati, progenitor of all life, as well as with Vishnu, preserver of life.

Even the tortoise's empty shell has found its way into myth. The Greek god Hermes invented the lyre by killing a tortoise and stretching strings of hide across its shell. He had to give the lyre to Apollo, whose symbol it became, as punishment for stealing Apollo's cattle. Because of its lustre and translucency when polished, tortoiseshell has long been prized as a material for making jewelry. For the Aztecs, the reflection of a human or a god's face distorted by the "panes" of the turtle's shell was a complex symbol of sensuality and untrustworthiness. Echoing its physical form, the animal in folk wisdom represented the bragging coward – hard on the outside yet soft within.

To early and medieval Christians the image of the tortoise was mundane. Carrying its home on its back and able to retreat in the face of a threat, the tortoise was a symbol of the modest woman living in her house.

A Mayan plate painted with the Earth turtle.

EARTH TURTLE

The Maya imagined the Earth as a large turtle. Although many Native Americans and peoples in the Old World shared this view, Mayan imagery was more elaborate than most. The turtle shell symbolized the rounded Earth out of which the maize god, Hun Hunahpu, was often portrayed emerging into the world. In the Mayan conception of world origins, where sacrifice, fertility and the underworld were all linked, the gods engaged in bloodletting rituals at an altar whose form was a monstrous turtle.

Sometimes the Mayans allied the turtle more closely with the watery surface that separates the earth from the sky, and then it was identified with the rain god Chac, whose various manifestations wore the turtle's shell in rain-bringing rituals.

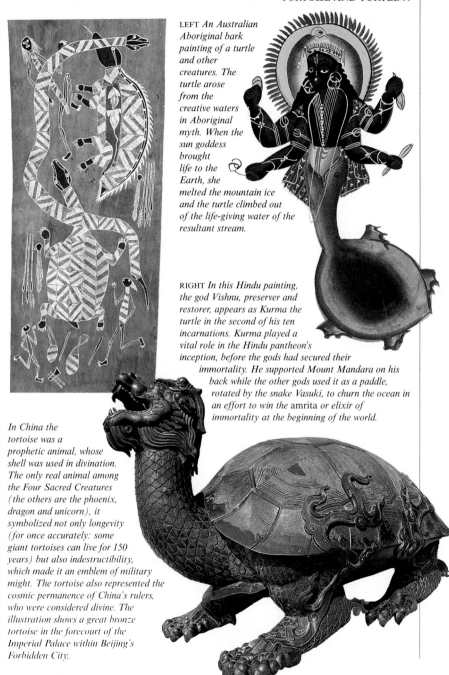

LEFT *An Australian Aboriginal bark painting of a turtle and other creatures. The turtle arose from the creative waters in Aboriginal myth. When the sun goddess brought life to the Earth, she melted the mountain ice and the turtle climbed out of the life-giving water of the resultant stream.*

RIGHT *In this Hindu painting, the god Vishnu, preserver and restorer, appears as Kurma the turtle in the second of his ten incarnations. Kurma played a vital role in the Hindu pantheon's inception, before the gods had secured their immortality. He supported Mount Mandara on his back while the other gods used it as a paddle, rotated by the snake Vasuki, to churn the ocean in an effort to win the* amrita *or elixir of immortality at the beginning of the world.*

In China the tortoise was a prophetic animal, whose shell was used in divination. The only real animal among the Four Sacred Creatures (the others are the phoenix, dragon and unicorn), it symbolized not only longevity (for once accurately: some giant tortoises can live for 150 years) but also indestructibility, which made it an emblem of military might. The tortoise also represented the cosmic permanence of China's rulers, who were considered divine. The illustration shows a great bronze tortoise in the forecourt of the Imperial Palace within Beijing's Forbidden City.

Crocodile, alligator and caiman

The caiman of Central and South America, the alligator of the southeastern United States and China, and the crocodile of Africa, Asia, Australia and Central America, are the largest surviving lizards, all primevally terrifying in appearance. Their habit of lying with jaws agape is innocent – they must use more muscles to close their jaws than to open them (Aristotle believed that the crocodile could not move its lower jaw at all) – but inspires understandable fear in human beings. All are ferocious hunters, and sometimes they take large prey, including deer, buffalo and humans. In early Christian belief, being eaten by a crocodile indicated a person had gone to Hell.

Being amphibious – able to live and hunt on water or land – crocodiles have been seen as archetypes of human ambiguity. Their eyes have nictitating membranes – or "third eyelids" – which protect them when swimming. These membranes also occasionally close over the open eyes of the basking reptiles, giving them a glazed appearance which must have made it seem to early observers that the crocodiles were weeping hypocritically for their prey. The dung of crocodiles was once widely used as a cosmetic to reduce facial wrinkles, a fact mentioned in medieval bestiaries, which therefore linked the crocodile with vanity, luxury and deceit.

The female Nile crocodile – the common African species – lays a clutch of up to 70 eggs in a nest underground, which she guards closely. When the young hatch, the mother digs them out and gently carries them to the water in her mouth. For many African peoples the crocodile has a cosmogonic fertility role, as well as being an ancestor spirit.

Aboriginal clan dancers at Aurukun in Australia re-enact the activities of the crocodile, one of their ancestors who lived in the Dreamtime – the period before human memory, when supernatural beings roamed the land.

The crocodile was thought by medieval writers to pretend to cry so as to lure passers-by within reach of its jaws. As a result, feigned tears are known as "crocodile tears" and have come to signify human deceit.

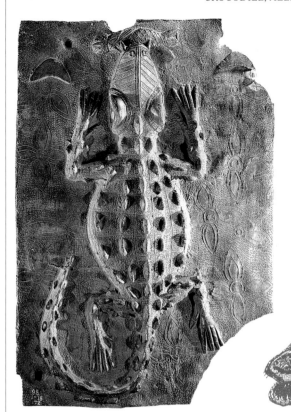

A 17th-century crocodile plaque which used to decorate the walls of the palace of the Oba of Benin in West Africa. The crocodile's liver and entrails are considered powerful magic in much of West Africa. They can be used by skilful witchdoctors to cast spells leading to death.

In Mexico the caiman, a relative of the alligator, was one of the most venerated carnivores. Among the Maya it was identified especially with the aged creator deity Itzamna.

SEBEK THE SACRED

Ancient Egyptians revered some crocodiles as sacred animals and mummified them accordingly when they died. The Greek geographer Strabo, *c.* 60BC–AD21, commented on the ritual feeding of a crocodile at the cult centre of Crocodilopolis. Promoted to the status of a deity as the crocodile god Sebek, the reptile was adorned with golden earrings and other jewels. In this form, he was thought to be essentially evil, and was linked to Set, god of the underworld, who had taken crocodile form after the murder of his brother Osiris. However, Sebek also had benevolent associations, as an ancient solar deity and a patron of the pharaohs, many of whom – for example, Sebek-hotep, meaning "Sebek is satisfied"– took his name as an additional title.

Serpent

Across the world and throughout human history, the serpent or snake has inspired more cults and mysteries than any other animal. It is a recurring motif in myth, art and religion, and its image is as supple as its body: it can symbolize life, death, rebirth, sacred knowledge and the afterlife.

Although limbless, snakes are often excellent climbers. Many species have powerful, prehensile tails, and large scales on their bellies can be tilted forward and back to drag them up tree trunks and branches.

On the ground, the zigzagging snake can penetrate narrow crevices and emerge without warning from dark tunnels. Such behaviour identifies it inevitably as a messenger from the underworld; for example, in ancient Greece the snake was seen as the incarnation of a departed soul.

In North America, traditional wisdoms perceive the snake as a spirit-messenger between the upper and lower worlds, and in many cultures worldwide serpents are associated with the Cosmic Tree, whose roots lie deep in the soil of the nether world, and whose trunk and branches reach toward the sun. The snake goddess of Minoan Crete is depicted on coins as sitting beneath a tree, caressing a serpent. In China the snake is one of the twelve animals of the zodiac which sit under the Twelve Terrestrial Branches of the Year Tree. For Christianity the serpent represents Satan when twining around the Tree of Knowledge, but Christ when depicted on the Tree of Life. Norse mythology tells of Nidhogg, the "Dread Biter", lying coiled around the roots of the World Tree Yggdrasil, threatening to devour the foundations of the world.

The serpent's association with death is emphasized in those myths where it is seen to embody the dark powers of the Earth in conflict with the light of the sun – as, for example, in the battle between Python and the Greek sun god Apollo. Similar imagery pervades the traditional lore of Sumatra, where it is believed that a cosmic snake which inhabits the nether regions will finally rise up to destroy the world.

In the Pacific Islands, however, the

Dancing with snakes is an ancient custom, found in Minoan and Mexican art as well as forming part of mystery rites on the Greek island of Samothrace. In Asia snake charming is still a common spectacle, although snakes cannot hear the music and are probably mesmerized by the swaying of the snake charmer's body. Danger is minimized by removing the snake's poison glands.

The Book of Genesis relates how the serpent caused humankind to be banished from the Garden of Eden (depicted above in a 12th-century mosaic from Monreale Cathedral in Sicily). God gave Adam and Eve freedom in the garden, forbidding them only to eat of the fruit of the Tree of Knowledge of good and evil. However, the serpent beguiled Eve into eating the fruit, and its punishment was to crawl through dust on its belly for all the days of its life.

serpent is associated with pregnancy as creator of the world, and for the Rio Indians the anaconda is a mythical ancestor who swam up the Amazon river and vomited the first people onto dry land. The ancient Greek and Egyptian figure of Ouroboros, the serpent biting its own tail, is a powerful symbol of the never-ending cycle of life, and a staff entwined with two serpents was the symbol of Asclepius, the Graeco-Roman god of medicine. Serpents can also be magical companions to Great Mother figures such as Ishtar, the Babylonian fertility goddess, and Ananta, the thousand-headed Hindu mistress of serpents.

Despite occasional fatalities, modern snake-handling cults persist in the Bible Belt of the southern United States. By

SERPENT POWER

For many pre-Columbian civilizations the serpent symbolized transformation and cosmic rebirth. The Aztec creator god Quetzelcoatl was a feathered serpent. More generally, the serpent was associated with water, fertility and the sky, and its jaws conceived of as the entrance to the underworld. In Mayan art, sacred ancestors manifested themselves as snakes when a ruler acceded to power. The snake is closely associated with sacrificial bloodletting rites, and this relief from the Mayan city of Yaxchilan portrays a "vision serpent" coiling up from blood-stained paper.

Guardian of the earth and sacred waters, the serpent played a central role in the religious life of Native Americans. It stands for eternity and magic power, and is the mediator between humankind and the underworld. The Serpent Mound (left), a sacred site to many Native Americans, winds for a quarter of a mile (0.5 km) along a hillside in Ohio. It is built in the form of a giant snake which holds the "cosmic egg" clamped in its jaws.

holding poisonous snakes followers attempt to prove their faith in God's ability to protect them. It has been suggested that the worshippers' trancelike state slows their circulation, which cools their hands and makes the cold-blooded reptiles sluggish and passive.

The snake's exaggerated phallic shape has also won it a role as a totem of male fertility. In India, the *linga*, a pillar which represents the phallus of the god Shiva, is guarded by cobras. Because of its deadliness, the cobra is especially revered in many cultures. The Hindu god Vishnu rode the cobra of wisdom, and Egyptian pharaohs wore the sacred *uraeus* (cobra) as a symbol of royalty and divinity in their crowns.

Symbol of both death and renewal, the venomous snake can kill with its bite, yet by sloughing its skin it gives the promise of rebirth. The custom of circumcision – the shedding of the foreskin from the phallus, which originated in Egypt – may have begun as a ritual of rebirth among snake cults. Circumcision marks the young male's passage from adolescence to manhood in many cultures worldwide.

SNAKE RITUALS

In Australian Aboriginal mythology the cosmic serpent Yurlunggur coils around the Wawilak Sisters and their sons, as in the bark painting below, before swallowing them into its primeval stomach. This mythical event is re-enacted as an initiation ritual. The men of a tribe take the boys to a sacred spot forbidden to women. When the boys return they are regarded as having been regurgitated by the serpent, and are thus reborn as men.

Frog, toad and salamander

Frogs and toads, members of the same family of tailless amphibians, share much of their traditional symbolism as creatures linked with the embryonic stages of life, fertility and the watery processes of birth and rainfall. Both were lunar animals, a symbolism associating their radical changes of shape from tadpole to adult with the changing phases of the moon. Amphibian metamorphosis probably created the reputation for infinite changeability that lies behind the folklore of frogs transforming themselves into princes. The toad, valuable in ecology as a consumer of insects, acquired a sinister reputation in the Near East, and later in Christian Europe, perhaps because it was poisonous. However, the Chinese made use of dried toad poison in ancient medical preparations, anticipating the use of serotin (secreted by the toad) to constrict blood vessels.

The frog also appears as a legendary creature in the Vedic myth that a giant frog supported the world – a metaphor for the primeval state of matter. In Aztec cosmology, the toad-like monster Tlaltecuhtli, which served as a symbol of the Earth, floated in the primeval sea, its gaping mouth ready to swallow the sun at dusk. In Egypt, the frog goddess, Hekt, protected new-born babies and embodied the power of the waters. The green Nile frog was an emblem of abundance. Both the frog with its mass of spawn and the toad with its strings of eggs were widespread symbols of fecundity and rainfall. The croaking of frogs presaged rain both in Mexico and in southeast Asia. Toads were also often widely linked (correctly) with longevity, and in China and Europe with wealth – hence images of toads with jewels in their foreheads.

For medieval Christians, toads were familiars of witches, symbols of avarice and lust, and tormenters of those in Hell for these and other sins. The link between licentious behaviour and the urgent grapplings of mating frogs and toads goes back at least to classical antiquity when the frog was an emblem of the goddess of love, Aphrodite. In Amazonia toads represented the female genitalia and were symbols of adultery.

THE SALAMANDER

A type of amphibian called the fire salamander – because of its bright orange-and-black markings – had the phoenix-like reputation of being born in fire and being able to withstand the fiercest flames. This Greek fable was disseminated by Pliny, who had a weakness for marvellous creatures. The story impressed Christian writers who used it as an allegory of the righteous quenching the flames of lust. As some tales depicted the salamander breathing flame like a dragon, it became a symbol in alchemy of fire itself and of sulphur, the purifying agents in alchemical processes. The heraldic salamander is used to represent courage. The real creature, found in Europe and parts of West Asia and North Africa is damp-loving and timid, although some species are noxious to predators.

This copy of a Navaho sand painting from Arizona shows white and yellow female frogs marking the north and south points of the compass, and black and blue male frogs in the east and west. The Navaho believe that frogs were people originally, who planted corn (shown in the quadrants) to feed themselves. The rainbow bars have both protective and fructifying significance.

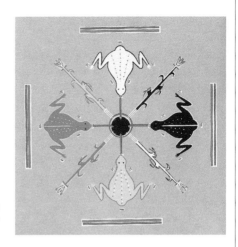

BELOW *A 19th-century Japanese print showing Gama Sennin, a toad magician. In Chinese mythology he had acquired immortality by the practice of asceticism. Gama Sennin was a companion to frogs and toads, and put his powers to practical use by selling drugs endowed with magic powers.*

ABOVE *The toad is linked with the moon, transformations and immortality in this mythical scene on the back of a Tang bronze mirror. The toad is Chang E who became goddess of the moon in this form. She had been promised a wonderful transformation if she went to the moon instead of to heaven after draining immortal elixir from a cup meant for herself and her husband. The bird, tortoise, dragon and tiger represent points of the compass, while the lunar hare is pounding the elixir of immortality.*

Spider and scorpion

Scorpions are purely destructive in most mythologies. Their poisonous stings are rarely fatal to humans, but can cause extreme pain. When hunting, many species run about at random, relying on touch to tell them when they have encountered their insect prey. In this way they have acquired a reputation for wanton aggressiveness. They are also excellently adapted to living in deserts, and suffer all the negative connotations of being associated with these wastelands. In the First Book of Kings of the Old Testament, the scorpion typifies drought, the wilderness, desolation

A 1,000-year-old shell disk with a spider from a Mississippian cult, Illinois. Images of the spider in Native American societies often serve as protective amulets against all that threatens their "webs" of life, both physical and spiritual.

and a dreadful scourge. Amazonian peoples believed that the scorpion was sent by a jealous creator to punish men for impregnating women whom he himself desired.

The reputation of the spider is more ambivalent. Its cunning, skill and industry are recognized, as well as its venom. Among many African cultures the artfulness of the web-spinners and the nimble movements of the hunter spiders have made them into trickster gods. In Greek mythology a Lydian maid, Arachne, challenged the goddess Athena to a weaving contest. Arachne filled her canvas with subjects that showed the failings of the gods. Athena tore the impious work to pieces and the terrified maiden hanged herself. Athena then turned Arachne into a spider and the rope into a cobweb, condemning the maid and her descendants to spin forever.

Many mythologies see the spider as a female force. The Tukano tribe of northwest Amazonia likened its web to the placenta, and Ixchel, the Mayan goddess of midwifery, took the form of a spider. The Great Weaver is also the Creator, who spins the thread of life from its own substance and attaches all people to it by this umbilical cord.

The spider is identified with the world-weaving Egyptian deity Neith. It is mistrusted as the weaver of the web of illusions by Hindus and Buddhists.

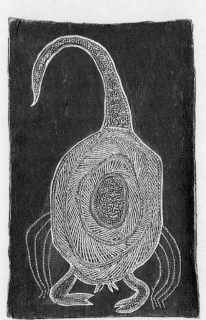

A scorpion from an Aboriginal bark painting of the 20th century, Groote Eylandt, Australia.

The spider, its poison-tipped chelicerae raised, forms part of a group of huge figures scratched into the surface of several desert mesas on the southern coast of Peru. The shapes, known as the Nazca Lines, were possibly etched in the 6th century AD and have been preserved by the extreme dryness of the climate. The scale of the figures is so huge that their form is virtually indecipherable from ground level but plainly visible from the air. Their purpose is not known, but they seem to have astronomical, calendrical or possibly religious significance.

SCORPION AND DEATH

The eighth sign of the zodiac, Scorpius, was sent to Earth to punish the vanity of the hunter, Orion, who boasted he could kill any animal on earth. Scorpius stung Orion to death.

The Egyptian god Set took the form of a scorpion for his attempt to murder the infant god of the sun, Horus. The Egyptians believed that a dead crocodile might turn into a scorpion.

The scorpion was commonly associated with destruction by the Mayans who occupied Central America from *c.*AD300–*c.*900.

In this scene from a Mayan vessel, the scorpion and serpent relate to rain, wind and storms, the three elemental destroyers.

Bat

As a nocturnal mammal and dweller in dark places, the bat was represented in many mythologies and religions as an enemy of light and therefore an ally or embodiment of evil spirits. As a flying mammal, capable of bird-like aerobatics but with a body like that of a shrew or mouse, it was also seen as a hybrid creature capable of supernatural transformations. Its unusual appearance includes fangs, large ears and prehensile feet which grip a perch so securely that the creature is able to sleep upside-down. Some species hibernate in this position, and bats in medieval bestiaries represented affection, because of their tendency to hang in closely bunched groups. However, the bat's other attributes, combined with its habit of flying in seemingly lunatic, erratic swoops at twilight, combined to breed nightmares in the human imagination.

In the Old Testament the bat was an abomination, and the New Testament calls it the "Devil's bird". Indeed, Christians saw the bat as an incarnation of Satan and the willing familiar of witches. The Devil (as well as other monsters) was depicted with bat-wings – thin skin stretched between the strut-like bones of hands and feet. Feathers (which were considered a more advanced adaptation for flight) were reserved for depicting more spiritual creatures. German countryfolk used to nail bats to doors to terrify the Devil, presumably by showing him what treatment he could expect should he appear in person. In Central American traditions, the bat appears as a mythical devourer of the sun. Bats were thought to flock around Mictlantecuhtli, the Aztec lord of the underworld, carrying severed human heads in their claws.

VAMPIRES

A Central and South American family of bats, *Desmodus*, bites sleeping birds and mammals and laps their blood, using salival anticoagulants to keep it flowing. The bites are relatively harmless because these bats are no bigger than the palm of a human hand, but they can transmit serious diseases including rabies. As most bats live not on blood but on insects, fruit or nectar, *Desmodus* aroused interest among European naturalists who called it the "vampire bat". The choice of name forged a ghoulish link with old superstitions about evil bats and Slavic folk legends

of blood-sucking vampires. These beings were reanimated corpses thought to live on the blood of sleeping human victims, who in turn became vampires as they were drained of life and died. Sensationalized Victorian illustrations of vampire bats, such as the example above, inspired Bram Stoker to update the vampire myth in his novel *Dracula* (1897) by making Count Dracula metamorphose into a terrifying giant bat.

These sinister associations were not universal. As its remarkable auditory senses, which allowed it to navigate in the dark with great precision, were mistaken for acute eyesight, the bat was a symbol of vigilance both in classical Greece and in parts of Africa. Homer associated bats with human souls, and so did some African and South American peoples. Pre-Columbian images produced by the Tairona people show a being combining bat and human features. In the mythology of their Kogi descendants, the bat (a creature that actually has a relatively short evolutionary history) is the first of the animals of creation, the product of the sun's incestuous love for his son. The bat also symbolizes menstruation and female fertility. In China, gifts were sent with a card showing a pair of bats. As the word *fu* (bat) also stands for good luck, the bats conveyed the Chinese recipe for happiness – health, wealth, longevity and an easy death.

A pre-Columbian Peruvian gold emblem, which was linked with sorcery, from Nazca.

All bats rely on their acoustic skills to navigate in darkness and find food. Many can pluck insects out of mid air, but this long-eared bat has gone in search of honeysuckle nectar. They "see" by echo location, sending out high-frequency clicks in a form of pulsed sonar which evolved millions of years before 1930s scientists hit upon the secrets of radar.

Owl

Familiar as a folk symbol of wisdom and (perhaps somewhat dusty) scholarship, the owl has attracted darker meanings in many ancient civilizations, especially China, where it was associated with thunder and the summer solstice. Owlets were believed in China to pluck out their mother's eyes.

The owl's night excursions, staring eyes and strange call have led to a widespread association with occult powers. The bird's superb night vision may underlie its connection with prophecy, and the reputation for being all-seeing could arise from its ability to turn its head through almost 180 degrees.

The owl was the bird of death in ancient Egypt, India, China, Japan, and Central and North America. In some regions, however, it had the role of supernatural protector – for example, among the Native Americans of the Plains, who wore owl feathers as magic talismans.

In ancient Athens the owl was made sacred to Athene Pronoia, goddess of wisdom, depicted on coins with an owl on the obverse side. From this Greek tradition comes the bird's association with sagacity.

Barn owls are fond of roosting in old, deserted buildings. The isolation of such places, often coupled with their reputation for being haunted, has undoubtedly contributed to the owl's popular association with ghosts and the supernatural. The owl's wing feathers are the softest of any bird, allowing it to fly in near silence so as to swoop unexpectedly on mice and other rodents. The extreme quietness of such a large bird can itself be eerie to humans. Although the owl has excellent eyesight, it locates much of its prey through an acute sense of hearing. Northern grey owls hunting in winter can hear the rustling of a single vole beneath a thick layer of snow.

Eagle, hawk and falcon

The long claws, strong talons, powerful hooked beak and swift, deadly strike of birds of prey have always endeared them to warrior classes, and to young, ambitious, aggressive civilizations, many of which have adopted the eagle as their national emblem. The Roman eagle, or *aquila*, was a figure of imperial might whose wings sheltered the *Pax Romana*. The ideals of the founders of the USA, influenced by Republican Rome, led them to choose the native bald eagle – named for its white head – as the symbol of their new country.

For the Aztecs the eagle was the "imperial bird", with its own elite warrior society, and its use by Nazi Germany emphasized the bird's predatory nature.

Within the USA, Native American symbolism of the northwest coast represented the eagle as the prototypical Thunderbird, whose cosmic clashes with spirits of the underworld were said to cause thunderstorms and earthquakes. When it was depicted on a clan's totem poles, it stood for the mythical founder of the clan.

Birds of prey have always been favoured hunting companions of the nobility, and have been connected with powerful and kingly gods around the world: Mithra (Persia), Indra (India), Zeus (Greece) and the Viking Odin.

The soaring eagle commands a view from horizon to horizon: to the Hittites it was the omniscient solar deity. In medieval Christian thought, it symbolized the spirit rising to heaven. The fishing eagle's dive into the ocean was seen as a form of baptism, and as Christ rescuing lost souls, although in the Old Testament the eagle was unclean, and was interchangeable with the vulture.

In the 12th century the Aztecs took the appearance of an eagle alighting on a cactus as a sign of where to site their capital city Tenochtitlan, which is now Mexico City (shown here in an illustration from a 16th-century book, the Codex Mendoza).

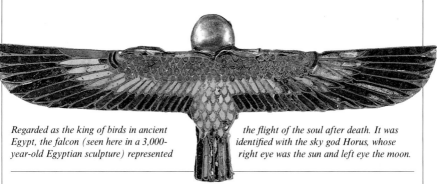

Regarded as the king of birds in ancient Egypt, the falcon (seen here in a 3,000-year-old Egyptian sculpture) represented   *the flight of the soul after death. It was identified with the sky god Horus, whose right eye was the sun and left eye the moon.*

FIGHTING EAGLE

Many eagle myths spread from the Hittite empire to Byzantium, and thence into Christian folklore. Mythological confrontations between the eagle and the lion or the eagle and the bull, in which the eagle is always victorious, symbolize the triumph of the spirit over brute force. When shown in battle with serpents, as in this medieval mosaic from Istanbul (below), the eagle represents the victory of celestial, spiritual powers over those of evil and darkness. Similarly, in Chinese philosophy the eagle is a fearless and tenacious warrior on the side of right. When not in conflict, the eagle and the serpent may together stand for totality and cosmic unity, as exemplified in the union of spirit and matter.

Raven and crow

With their black plumage and distinctive throaty calls, the raven and crow are associated with mortality, bereavement and war in western Europe, but elsewhere their symbolic character is often more benevolent. In China, for example, the raven was the three-legged symbol of the Chou dynasty, suggesting the rising, zenith and sinking of the sun. The bird's solar connotations are widespread, even though in the most superficial weavings of the folk imagination it qualifies so well as a metaphor of darkness. At a more esoteric level, the underlying assumption may be that its blackness, offering protection from the sun's heat, fits the creature well for solar companionship.

In Biblical imagery the raven is often deeply negative, but sometimes appears in a more positive light. It took bread and meat to Elijah in the wilderness, and its benevolence to such Christian saints as Bernard and Cuthbert, to whom it offered food and advice, led to its adoption as a symbol of holy solitude.

Among the raven's most elaborate supernatural imagery is that invented by the Inuit of Siberia and Alaska, who believe that Raven came from the primeval darkness and stayed to teach the first humans how to survive. Killing a raven, the representative of the creator god, would bring foul weather. Similarly, for the Native Americans of the northwest Pacific coast, Raven was a transformer, cosmic trickster (see p.44) and culture hero – the bringer of light and fire. From Alaska to British Columbia, a vast oral cycle of narrative traces the vivid, sometimes violent, adventures of this alternately ingenious and dim-witted bird-human, as it travels the world in a voracious quest for food and sex.

The croak of the raven and crow led to their identification as "talking birds" – messengers of the other world, endowed with the gift of prophecy. The

An early 19th-century French political cartoon showing France torn apart by internal political factions, represented as crows. The image recalls some medieval bestiaries, in which crows blinded sinners by pecking out their eyes with their strong beaks – a vivid symbol of "penance".

Viking war god Odin owned two magical ravens, one representing "thought", the other "memory": they would fly out into the world and bring back news. The identification of the raven as watchful messenger and prophet is also seen in ancient Greek myth. Originally the bird was said to have been white, but its constant chattering and propensity to bring evil tidings made its feathers grow ever darker. It was believed to have foretold the deaths of Plato and Cicero. In Rome the crow's hoarse call sounds like the Latin *cras* ("tomorrow"), making it a symbol of hope.

In Celtic lore also the raven was a creature of augury, and appears as Badhbh, the "Raven of Battle", as well as Morrigán, the raven war goddess.

Aboriginals of southeastern Australia believed that Crow, together with Eaglehawk, sorted out the degrees of kinship legitimate in marriage and outlawed incest. There is an echo of this notion in Christian theology, where the crow could symbolize fidelity within the family. However, it was also the spirit familiar of witches and the symbol of those who refused a Christian burial. Identified with the Devil, its depiction as a feeder on corruption reflected its natural behaviour as a bird of carrion.

RAVEN AS CREATOR

"In the beginning, Raven made us, and everything, and totem poles too."

So say the peoples of the northwest coast of America, for whom the raven is a significant mythic figure, the great creator or transformer of the world.

A myth of the Haida (Queen Charlotte Islands) tells of the raven finding a giant clam on a beach at Naikun as the waters of the great flood receded. The clam was full of terrified little creatures. Raven persuaded them to leave their shell and explore the world, and eventually they grew to become the first people. The story is depicted in the modern wood carving by Bill Reid (right).

Other myths of the northwest American coast tell of Raven stealing the sun, and bringing the first salmon, berries and other gifts to humankind.

Stork

The stork has a remarkably consistent set of positive and benevolent symbolic attributes across many different cultures. The announcer of spring, it is also in Christian lore Christ's herald. If a stork chooses to build its nest on the roof of a building in Europe, this is still considered a good omen. (Storks nest on chimneys and church spires in parts of northern and eastern Europe, and notably in the town of Cácares, Extramadura, in south-central Spain.)

In ancient Greece the stork was sacred to the goddess Hera (protector of nursing mothers), which is probably the origin of the Western folk belief that storks bring babies. Because storks were thought to care for their aged progenitors as well as their own offspring, there are also associations with filial piety – for example, in China. Another connection, widespread in the East, is with longevity (which in Taoism becomes extended to immortality). Christian lore links the stork with purity, piety and resurrection.

A white stork in flight. The stork's association with the fertile waters of creation echoes the story of the bird bringing newborn babies into the world. According to legend the children are embryos in the cosmic waters, and are discovered by the stork as it searches for fish.

The stork's natural skill at fishing extends to its habit of preying on reptiles, and it can be deft at catching snakes with its bill. The image of the stork killing snakes, widespread in art, relates to the solar and fire symbolism of the stork's red head.

Crane

Like many birds, the crane was often portrayed as a divine messenger, and in China it was envisaged as conveying the souls of the dead to the Western Paradise. When depicted in flight towards the sun, it was also for the Chinese a symbol of social ambition.

Vigilance, longevity, wisdom and fidelity are prominent in the spectrum of the creature's positive attributes. The bird's large and powerfully built wings metaphorically bestowed on it the ability to reach higher levels of spiritual consciousness. Christians attributed to it various benign qualities, including the virtues of the ordered monastic life.

In contrast to the wholly benevolent stork, however, the crane's symbolic character is not entirely spotless. In India it connoted treachery, and in some Celtic areas it was thought to be a creature of ill omen.

The crane is a bird of the wetlands, and its habit of standing on one leg and tucking up the other in its feathers generated a belief in the classical world that cranes made use of sentries among them when they slept. The sentry bird supposedly held a stone in its raised foot, so that if it lost consciousness the stone would drop on to its other foot and waken it.

The ancient Greeks believed that the V-shape of the cranes' migratory flight formation, with experienced birds leading and shielding younger members of the group, offered a useful social lesson. The Holy Roman Emperor, Frederick II, was the first to note, in the 13th century, that cranes actually take turns at leading the formation. Their cries on migration were taken as a signal for the spring sowing and the autumn reaping.

ABOVE *In Chinese thought the crane was a symbol of felicity and immortality: it was thought to live for a thousand years or more. Pure white cranes, shown here on a 16th-century Chinese blue and white porcelain vase, were believed to be especially sacred.*

LEFT *Cranes were venerated in Japan and addressed as "Honorable Lord". As in China, they were credited with immensely long lifespans. The elegance of their natural lines made them popular subjects with Japanese artists, as in this print of c.1830.*

Peacock

The peacock's tail (more strictly, rump ornament) of iridescent "eyed" feathers fanned out to attract the hen gives the bird a shimmering grandeur. This in itself explains the creature's identification with solar glory, royalty and immortality; moreover, its flesh was thought to be incorruptible.

In ancient India and, later, Iran the wheel-like tail motif was a symbol of the all-seeing sun and the eternal cosmic cycle. As the bird became better known farther west, it came to represent rebirth, the starry heavens, and the unity of the cosmos.

According to Hindu belief it was the cosmic mount of Kama the god of love, and the sacred animal of Sarasvati, goddess of wisdom and poetry. Its associations with nobility and dignity are evident in China, where the gift of a peacock's feather was a sign of imperial favour, and in Iran, where the court revolved around the "Peacock Throne".

In Greek mythology, Pan gave a peacock to Hera, who sprinkled its tail with the hundred eyes of the slain giant Argos. In Buddhism, as the emblem of Avalokiteshvara, the bird connotes compassionate watchfulness.

Although Christian iconography portrays the peacock's tail as both a halo and the all-seeing eyes of the Church, puritanical thought undermined its status, associating it with pride and vanity. This theme occurs satirically in secular imagery, as in this 15th-century relief from the school of Leonardo (above). Elsewhere, the peacock stood for luxury, as in this medieval Persian painting (right).

Cockerel

Famous for its dawn call, the cock or rooster has come to symbolize solar and spiritual resurrection. In Greek mythology it was dedicated to Apollo and identified with Persephone as the returning spring. In Judaism, similar associations with fertility held the cock and hen to be symbols of the bridal couple at weddings. Christian church weathervanes in the form of cocks are emblems of watchfulness against evil, and in Christianity generally the associations are positive (rebirth, the defeat of spiritual ignorance) despite a tradition linking the bird with lust.

Throughout China the white cockerel protects the innocent against evil spirits, and symbolizes the purity of new life overcoming death; while the red cock wards off fire. In the Shinto belief of Japan, the cockerel's arousing cry represents the call to prayer, and the bird is frequently shown standing on a drum in the religious imagery of temple architecture. There is a mythical parallel between the call to prayer and the cock calling Amaterasu, the sun goddess, out of the cave in which she hides her light. Cocks are sacred animals in Japan, and run free in the temples.

Christ foretold that Peter would deny him three times before the cock crowed, as depicted in this mid 15th-century fresco by Giacomo Giaquerio. Hence in Christian thought the bird represents the sinner's human weakness.

The cock is also venerated in Islamic belief, as in this 20th-century embossed painting: it was the huge bird that Mohammed saw in the first heaven crowing "There is no god but Allah". The rooster's "cocksure" supremacy in the farmyard has led to its linkage with virility, courage and pugnacity. In Celtic and Nordic lore the cock is an otherworldly messenger, escorting souls, calling the dead to battle, warning the gods of danger.

Goose and swan

These large web-footed water birds are sufficiently alike in biology and behaviour to have been treated similarly in myth. Many species migrate, and in flight, in their distinctive "V" formation, these muscular birds make a stirring spectacle. Their aerial majesty links them both to the otherworld.

In Siberia these are shamanic creatures. The swan, which symbolizes the shaman's immersion in the underworld, was the guiding spirit of the first shaman according to the Tungus. Similarly the migrating goose, as spirit-helper, carries the shaman on celestial adventures, during which the shaman imitates the bird's clamorous calls to announce his departure and return.

The swan is a complex symbol of light, death, shape-shifting, beauty and melancholic passion. It has male, solar connotations (as in the Germanic legend of Lohengrin), but also appears as the personification of feminine grace and beauty (*Swan Lake*). In ancient Greece the swan was a master of spirit flight through its identification with Hermes, the divine messenger of the Olympian gods. The recurrent theme of transformation in swan symbolism is adumbrated in the myth of the seduction of Leda.

The Greek belief that the swan made sweet music just once before it died persisted through Western culture, becoming especially potent in the age of Romanticism, when doom and creativity made a suggestively poetic mix. In an earlier period the swan-song was equated with the Christian martyrs affirming their faith before execution.

Geese, which make excellent alarms when disturbed, were kept sacred for Mars, the Roman god of war. In Celtic lore, too, the goose had military associations. The wild goose was a masculine, solar symbol in China, but also (as in Japan) the lunar bird of autumn.

In ancient Egypt the Nile goose, seen here in a 4th-dynasty pyramid fresco, was the "great chatterer", the creator bird which laid the "cosmic egg" from which Amun-Ra was hatched.

For the ancient Greeks the swan was the sacred bird of Aphrodite, the goddess of love, whose chariot was pulled by a brace of swans. The story of Leda and the swan (shown here in a painting which is probably a 16th-century copy of a work by Leonardo da Vinci) fixed the amorous connotations of swan symbolism for centuries to follow. Zeus took the bird's dazzling form to seduce the beautiful Leda, who later produced four children from two eggs – Clytemnestra, Castor, Pollux and Helen. Ironically, among ornithologists, the swan is widely known for its fidelity and often mates for life, pining away if its partner dies.

THE HAMSA

The goose and the swan are mythically interchangeable in Hinduism, as in many cultures. The Hamsa is one bird made of two, Ham and Sa, and it can appear as either a goose or a swan. It represents the perfect union, the "balance of life".

Brahma himself, the creator god, was born of the "cosmic egg" laid by this sacred bird (a mirroring of Egyptian mythology: see left). Sometimes the Hamsa is a form taken by Brahma.

Alternatively, it serves as his mount, as in this Indian painting (right) showing Brahma. (Brahma appears here with four heads, one for each of the four successive ages of the creation cycle.) The flight of the Hamsa represents the yearning of the soul for its release from the perpetual round of existence.

Hindu belief recognizes Sarasvati, Brahma's wife, as riding the swan. As Paramahasa, the Self is symbolized as the Supreme Swan.

Dove

Today the dove is treated everywhere as an emblem of peace, yet there is little in its somewhat argumentative nature to support such an interpretation. Its symbolism derives more from its luminous beauty and, in the West, the persuasiveness of Biblical references.

In Biblical and other contexts, the dove is a messenger: the bird returns to Noah with an olive leaf to indicate reconciliation between God and mankind. Redolent with renewal of life, this image is also the emblem of the Greek goddess Athena, and echoes more obliquely the myth of the dove feeding the infant Zeus with ambrosia. Dove symbolism in Christianity is extensive, ranging from the Holy Spirit (especially at the Annunciation) to chastity

A stained-glass window depicting a pair of doves. Quite apart from their religious connotations, two doves together are an emblem of conjugal contentment.

(despite ancient undercurrents of lasciviousness) and the purified soul.

In China the dove was associated with the Earth Mother and hence fertility, as well as with longevity. In Japan a dove bearing a sword announced the cessation of war.

This Byzantine mosaic in St Mark's Basilica, Venice, shows Noah releasing a dove from the Ark to fly over the floodwaters and scout for dry land. On its second foray it returned with a recently unfurled olive leaf, signifying that life was returning to a purified earth.

Quetzal and hummingbird

These birds of the Americas have attracted a body of symbolism that owes much to the brilliance of their plumage.

The rarely glimpsed quetzal bird (right) was especially prized by the Aztecs, for whom the male's two long curving tail feathers, shimmering in the rainforest with gilded emerald tinged with exquisite violet, were "the shadows of the sacred ones" and symbols of fertility. A major god in the Aztec and Toltec pantheon, Quetzalcoatl, the plumed serpent, incorporated the quetzal into his name and made his cloak from its feathers.

The hummingbird, which owes its name to the vibration of its rapidly beating wings as it hovers to collect nec-

tar, was linked by the Aztecs with Huitzilopochtli, the god of war: an attribution derived from its aggressive behaviour (it has been recorded as attacking creatures many times its own size). The only bird able to fly backwards as well as forwards, the hummingbird was thought to be a messenger to and from the gods. It symbolized rebirth, beauty, joy and speed, and its shining feathers were used as a love charm.

Sacred to the people who lived on the margins of the great Pitch Lake in Trinidad, the hummingbird supposedly took the first seeds of tobacco from the island to mainland South America.

A hummingbird carved out of the brown earth of the Nazca desert in Peru about two thousand years ago is one of the many mysterious giant landscape designs which have been interpreted as sacred pathways linking the shrines of the Nazca peoples.

Huitzilopochtli, the Aztec war god, is depicted in this codex illustration wearing a hummingbird head-dress and other accoutrements. In Nahuatl, the Aztecs' language, his name means "hummingbird of the left" or "hummingbird of the south".

Bee

Honeybees have been kept for their sugary food for several thousand years, and their combs were plundered for wild honey long before that. Apart from the significance of honey as the major source of sugar in the ancient world, honeycombs were the most important source of the beeswax that was widely used in making candles. Symbolic associations with light, and the golden colour of honey, made the bee a solar insect in Egypt, born from the tears of the sun god Ra.

The Egyptians and many other peoples drew lessons from the communal organization of bees, with workers transporting nectar and pollen, building and cleaning combs, feeding the young and fiercely guarding the hive. Bees were emblems not only of diligence and courage but also of less obvious spiritual and even political virtues. The queen bee (once mistaken for a king) was a symbol of royalty. As winged "beings of fire", bees were associated with purity and represented souls in many Middle Eastern traditions and from Siberia through central Asia to Bengal. As a Christian funerary motif, the bee symbolizes the resurrected soul.

Prehistoric communal houses on the island of Crete have a hive-like structure. In Greece, Zeus himself was said to have been nurtured by bees, and the priestesses of the Great Mother goddess Demeter at Elusius were called bees. The beehive became a Christian metaphor for the ordered, chaste and charitable life of monastic communities. A misconception that bees (which actually mate in massive swarms on the wing) reproduce as chastely as the flowers they pollinate made them emblems of the Virgin Mary. However, the Chinese linked bees with fickleness. In a poetic image of buzzing desire, the Hindu god of love, Kama, appears with a bowstring formed of bees. In Indian art, Vishnu is portrayed as a bee on a lotus, Shiva a bee above a triangle.

Wild honey was regarded as a food of the gods; and mead, based on fermented honey mixed with water, was drunk ritually with similar meaning both in the Celtic world and in Mali. Honey was also associated with eloquence, as in Greek legends that poets and orators such as Homer, Pindar, Sappho and Sophocles had their lips touched with honey in infancy.

The soothing properties of honey have long been recognized, as demonstrated by this honey-collecting scene from a 15th-century herbal. The bear profiting from the spillage suggests that even brute animals can be pacified by the influence of honey.

The decoration on this ancient Greek amphora of men beating off a swarm of stinging bees indicates that techniques of quietening bees took time to develop. In Christian allegory, the sweetness of honey and the sting of collecting it became a metaphor for the nature of Jesus himself and the agony of his Passion. In ancient Mexico, honey and wax were gathered from stingless bees. Bee-gods such as Ah Mucan Cab were patrons of Mayan beekeeping.

BEEKEEPING

Honeybees evolved as social insects step by step with the flowers they help to pollinate. They make honey by extracting water from the nectar and pollen they bring back to the comb, increasing the sugar content to 80 per cent. In Spain, cave paintings dating back 8,000 years show scenes of people collecting honey. Evidence of bee-keeping dates from 2400BC in the sun-temple of Neuserre, Egypt. Early hives in cylinders of mud or bark meant that colonies were destroyed when honey was collected. Systems were devised only gradually to remove the comb without disturbing the bees. The common honeybee is only one of thousands of bee species, mostly solitary rather than social.

Apis mellifera, *the honeybee*

Butterfly

The butterfly's metamorphosis from caterpillar to pupa to winged creature has turned it into a near-universal symbol of the soul and an evocative image of mystical rebirth. In much Christian imagery the butterfly emerging from the chrysalis represents the soul leaving the body at death. Australian Aboriginals regard butterflies as the returning spirits of the dead who have previously taken the form of caterpillars to reach the afterlife.

In Aztec Mexico the butterfly was associated with women who died in childbirth. Such women received the same glory as warriors who had fallen in battle, and it was perhaps because of this association that the butterfly goddess Itzpapalotl became a bloodthirsty deity, demanding regular sacrifice.

Although some butterflies hibernate, most live only a few weeks, but as an emblem of rebirth the butterfly has also come to represent longevity and immortality to the Maori of New Zealand, a view shared in China where it is also connected with the pleasures of living, its ceaseless, erratic movements signifying high spirits. In modern usage, however, "to be a butterfly" denotes someone who cannot concentrate on one thing and is thus never satisfied. Such imagery invokes ideas of inconstancy, especially in love. In Japan the butterfly symbolizes a false lover, a vain woman or a Geisha, and in Latin America the Spanish word for butterfly, *mariposa*, can refer to a prostitute, moving from one man to another.

Associations between the brightly coloured butterfly, "painted woman", passion and inconstancy are encapsulated in the Greek myth of Psyche, personification of the soul, whose name also means "butterfly". Her beauty ensnared Eros, the god of love, himself.

BELOW *A gold ornament from the city of Mycenae. The butterfly represented the Great Mother. In anthropomorphic form it symbolized the all-pervasive wisdom and procreative powers which the deity held within herself.*

ABOVE *A 1,500-year-old, partly reconstructed wall painting from Tepantitla, Mexico. The scenes are thought to represent the heaven of the rain god, Tlaloc. These are the souls who have pleased him, and they are in a state of bliss.*

ABOVE *This 20th-century represen-tation of butterflies in stained glass by John Piper is from a church window in Nettlebed, Oxfordshire, England. The butterfly's distinctive life-cycle symbolizes the human stages of life, death and resurrection.*

LEFT *Some species of butterfly are migratory, and may travel thousands of miles in swarms numbering several millions. This mass gathering takes place every year in the forests of northern Mexico. In pre-Columbian Mexico the dancing of a flame reminded the Aztecs of the quivering of butterflies' wings, and consequently the butterfly was viewed as a symbol of fire.*

Seal and walrus

Seals and walruses play a role in the world-view of the Inuit peoples of the Arctic, who pursue sea mammals in winter and spring, and move inland for the summer and autumn to concentrate

on caribou, fish and birds. In such societies, the seal and the walrus have a special relationship with the hunter, based on a mutual compact. Prey is not simply "taken", but permits itself to be killed. Commonly Inuit throw the bladders of seals and walruses, thought to possess their souls, back into the sea to be reborn as living creatures which will offer themselves as prey in the future.

On the northwest coast of America the seal bestowed its swimming and fishing skills on men. It also had a more sinister role: a seal's stomach filled with its blood was substituted for human flesh in an act of symbolic cannibalism whereby members of the community appeased evil spirits.

Seals and walruses figure in some cultures as primordial ancestors, capable of assuming human form. Their ability

to function on both land and sea offers a tempting but undoubtedly over-simplistic provenance for such transitions from the world of spirit to the world of matter. In fact, there are many species of seal (such as the ringed seal) whose rear flippers cannot pivot forwards (as a walrus's can), so that their locomotion on land is ungainly. More resonant is the image of the seal emerging through its breathing-hole in the ice – a sudden apparition from a world inaccessible to humankind. Some Inuit use the soft down feather of the eider, tied to the end of a stick, as a signal to reveal the seal's exhalations.

Folklore preserves echoes of seals taking human appearance, often for mating purposes. Scottish men could marry such seal-women as long as they kept their pelts hidden from them, to prevent their return to the sea.

In the Graeco-Roman tradition, it was believed that the seal's skin offered protection against thunderstorms, as the seal was never struck by lightning.

WALRUS TUSKS

Both sexes of the walrus have long tusks (upper canine teeth), which in the male can weigh up to 12lb (5.4kg) each and attain a length of about 3 feet (1m). In the Arctic, walrus ivory is a popular medium for incised decoration: this engraved ivory snow-knife (below) dates from the 19th century. An excavation on a Punuk site on Saint Lawrence Island in the Bering Sea in the 1920s revealed more than a hundred items made from walrus ivory, including a pin to prevent a seal from bleeding and a tensioning device for tent lines.

ABOVE *The elephant seal (or "sea elephant") derives its name from the male's inflatable snout, used for aggressive display. Male elephant seals may fight to the death for territorial and sexual supremacy (they have harems of up to 30 cows).*

RIGHT *An Inuit storage box representing a seal. The face on the lid is supposed to be the seal's soul. The Inuit believe that each person or animal has a number of different souls, and one of these is the defining soul of its species.*

Whale

The whale is now almost extinct because of the greed of humans in the 19th and 20th centuries. Although whales are warm-blooded mammals like ourselves, giving birth to live young, humans have treated them as the most alien of beings. During the 20th century the blue whale, the largest creature ever to inhabit the planet, has been reduced from a population of half a million to probably fewer than a hundred in order to make pet food and corset stays, perfume and cosmetics. In Japan, every year a ceremony intended to lift the curse placed on humankind for killing so many whales takes place at the Koganji Temple. The temple is dedicated to dead whales and faces the sea so that living whales can pay homage to their ancestors.

An Inuit mask skilfully blends the whale's form with a man's face so that the thrashing tail also depicts a convincing moustache. The Inuit have great respect for the intelligence of the whale, and considerable care is taken not to offend the creature's spirit.

Societies that depend on the whale for their livelihood have accorded it a respected place in mythology and ritual life. The Inuit of Alaska hold whaling ceremonies in which they decorate their canoes with scenes of hunters attacking whales. Their shamans wear ceremonial masks depicting whale spirits, and the wife of the officiating shaman draws whale flukes on her husband's chest. If a hunt is to be successful, the shaman's spirit helper emerges from his mouth in the form of a whale's fluke.

According to medieval Christian tradition, the whale was in league with the devil since it allegedly pandered to the senses by emitting a sweet-smelling scent to attract fish. For the Kwakiutl people of Vancouver Island the whale has a positive image as a bestower of long life and prosperity.

The haunting sounds that mariners heard long ago through the hulls of their wooden ships are now known to be the complex "songs" of whales communicating with each other across hundreds of miles of ocean. The half-hour song of the humpback whale contains a million information-carrying changes of frequency. It is the single most elaborate vocal display in the natural world.

THE TRIALS OF JONAH

The whale is famous in Judaeo-Christian thought for its part in the Biblical story of Jonah. God ordered Jonah to prophesy doom to the city of Nineveh but Jonah tried to evade his mission by fleeing on a ship. He was thrown overboard by sailors and was then swallowed by a "great fish". He emerged still alive after three terrifying days. According to Christians, the whale's jaws represented the gates of Hell and its interior the infernal region. Jonah's escape was interpreted as a symbolic resurrection and rebirth.

A detail from a 13th-century stained glass window.

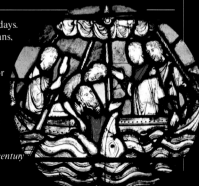

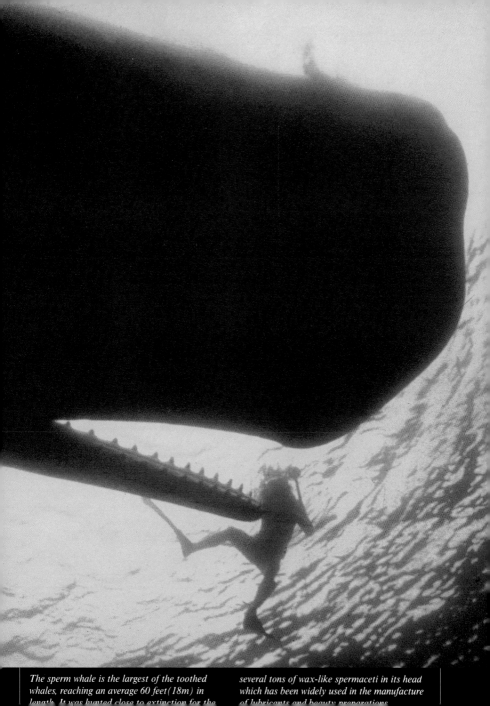

The sperm whale is the largest of the toothed whales, reaching an average 60 feet (18m) in length. It was hunted close to extinction for the several tons of wax-like spermaceti in its head which has been widely used in the manufacture of lubricants and beauty preparations.

Dolphin

Both dolphins and porpoises belong to the same family of toothed whales as the larger pilot whales and killer whales. Although dolphins and porpoises can be difficult to tell apart, in general the dolphins are larger, more streamlined and have more pronounced beaklike snouts. These snouts, with their apparently perpetual smiles, are one reason why humans have always shown such affection for dolphins. There are also, however, more rational and well-founded reasons.

The seeming altruism of dolphins' behaviour toward humans has profoundly influenced our attitudes to them. All over the world, dolphins have appeared, in both myths and factually verified accounts, rescuing swimmers or guiding ships through treacherous waters. In parts of the Mediterranean and along the coast of Brazil, partnerships still exist between fishermen and dolphins, which locate shoals of fish and may even drive them to the fishermen's nets. Dolphins and boys are often paired in Western art, and in modern times dolphins have appeared repeatedly as companions of swimming youths.

The belief that dolphins are linked to humankind by some form of spiritual kinship is common to many cultures, from the ancient Greeks to the Aboriginal people of northern Australia. Nabataen Arabs believed that dolphins accompanied the souls of the dead on their journey to the underworld. For many Native Americans dolphins were messengers between the real and spirit worlds, and embodied the Great Spirit. The dolphin's role as spiritual mediator was adapted by early Christians, for whom a dolphin impaled on a trident or hung on a cross was a secret symbol of Christ. In antiquity, it was widely believed that many cultures imposed the death penalty on anybody who killed a dolphin.

In Greek tradition, dolphins stood for love and salvation or spiritual rebirth. For the Minoan civilization of Crete, the dolphin incarnated the spirit of Poseidon, god of the sea. It was closely linked both with the solar god Apollo and with the female, water-born love goddess Aphrodite. In this way the dolphin symbolized the joining of the masculine (solar) world with the feminine, aquatic environment of the womb, a connection emphasized by the phonetic similarity between dolphin (*delphis*) and womb (*delphys*). Apollo was said to have changed himself into a dolphin to carry worshippers to his shrine at Delphi. In another story, Dionysus turned pirates into dolphins, which thereby became redeemed souls.

PLAYFUL NATURES

The brain of the dolphin is fully as complex as that of humans, although it evolved much earlier – some 20 million years ago. However, it works in a completely different way. Whereas the human brain is built for manipulating symbols, and for decision-making based on a fairly meagre sensory input, the bulk of the dolphin's brain is given over to interpreting huge quantities of sensory information resulting from a three-dimensional sonar-based appreciation of the world. It has even been suggested that the dolphin's brain constructs a constantly evolving hologram of its surroundings.

Dolphins show their intelligence through their playfulness. They are often seen surfing on the bow-waves of ships, and even in the wild engage in displays of synchronized leaping and acrobatics. In captivity, performing dolphins need little training. They are merely encouraged to follow their own instincts.

Swimming at speeds of up to 25mph (40 km per hour), dolphins may leap out of the water completely when they surface to breath. In this way they minimize drag and are able to maintain their speed.

According to the Greek writer Herodotus, the dolphin (Delphinus in the 1822 English star chart, above) was placed among the stars by Poseidon as a reward for saving Arion, a bard threatened with death by sailors. After delaying his attackers with a song, Arion threw himself into the sea and a dolphin carried him to safety.

In ancient Greece and Rome dolphins were associated with the Titan Oceanus, shown on this 4th-century silver plate. Oceanus was one of the elemental forces that brought the world into being.

Salmon and carp

The life-cycle of the salmon is almost as much of a mystery to modern science as it was to the Native Americans and Celts who once worshipped the fish. Salmon make huge migratory journeys, from the rivers and streams where they are born, into the open sea. There they mature before returning to the rivers of their birth to spawn. It is thought that the salmon's migrations are triggered by hormonal changes which modify its metabolism to create a need first for salt water, then for fresh water again when the time comes to spawn. The salmon probably navigates by the sun until it enters familiar coastal waters, and then uses its phenomenal sense of smell to locate the precise river of its birth. Neither of these theories is proven. Atlantic salmon may return repeatedly to the headwaters of their natal streams, but their Pacific counterparts, which include massive species weighing up to 80lb (35kg), return only once, in their millions, to spawn and die. They can travel thousands of miles upstream to reach their objective, the king salmon leaping several times its own body-length to scale cascades. To Native Americans of the northwest coast, the determination of these fish, their apparent fatalism and their sudden, annual superabundance, made them totemic

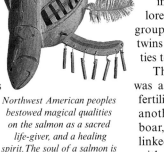

Northwest American peoples bestowed magical qualities on the salmon as a sacred life-giver, and a healing spirit. The soul of a salmon is represented in this 19th-century Alaskan mask. The pendants are stylized abstractions and reductions of the fish shape and reinforce the mask magic.

animals representing death and rebirth, fecundity, virility, courage, purposeful wisdom and foresight. Along the coast, "First Salmon" ceremonies included speeches welcoming the first schools of the year, dances to entertain the fish and the distribution of fishbones back to the salmon villages beneath the waves, to ensure the following year's bounty.

Pairs of leaping salmon suggested to the Kwakiutl of Vancouver Island that human twins might be transformed salmon – and needed to be kept away from water in case they changed back into fish form. In the lore of a neighbouring group, the Tsimshian, twins have magical abilities to call forth salmon.

The leaping salmon was a Celtic phallic and fertility symbol and, like another delicacy, the boar, the salmon was linked in druidic lore with spiritual wisdom and prescience. Both Celtic and Nordic traditions also connected salmon with human or divine transformations, and the migration of the soul. The trickster god Loki once fled Thor's wrath by changing into a salmon – one of many myths linking fish with the idea of liberty or escape. Fish were immune, for example, from the universal floods which feature in the myths of various peoples from Israel to the Arctic.

THE CARP

The carp lives in muddy lakes and slow rivers, and needs little oxygen, which has made it a popular species to cultivate because many fish can be kept in a small pond. Carp, which can live nearly 50 years, were Chinese symbols of longevity and perseverance, especially associated with literary skill and scholarship. They also brought good luck, and paper replicas of them were hung up to avert house fires. In Japan, the carp was an emblem of Samurai fortitude.

LEFT *Sadatora's 19th-century painting of a carp – the ancestor of many species of decorative fish, including the goldfish.*
BELOW *A 19th-century Japanese sword guard shows Kannon, goddess of compassion, riding the carp of courage.*

A salmon that has been killed and ceremonially prepared by northwestern Native Americans is addressed by them as if it were a high-ranking chief. Images of salmon were carved on totem poles, as in this detail from Wrangell, Alaska.

Shark

A silent and streamlined predator, the shark excites a strongly emotional response as a creature drawn to blood, embodying the universal fear of the dangers that lurk out of sight. Sharks circle their quarry, materializing seemingly out of nowhere, often attacking from below. On Australian, South African and New Zealand coastlines, lookout towers, bells, nets and sirens testify to a justified anxiety. The species most feared by humans (and the greatest menace along the shores of California) is the great white shark. Other potential threats to people include the tiger, bull, blue, hammerhead and oceanic white tip sharks. Many aspects of sharks' lives remain a mystery, because these animals are difficult to study in the wild, and this has tended to magnify the fear inspired.

Like most species, nurse sharks will attack humans when provoked, although given the opportunity they usually flee. Nurse sharks are especially common around the channels that run from coral reefs.

From the earliest times sharks have inspired accounts of man-eating sea monsters. It is sometimes thought that the Biblical story of Jonah relates to the shark rather than to the whale. Similar tales come from classical antiquity: for example, the account in the 5th century BC by Herodotus, who described how 300 Persians were eaten by sharks when Xerxes' invasion fleet was wrecked off Mount Athos in northern Greece. In the 16th century the complete body of a sailor was found inside a great white shark. However, the largest of all sharks, the 50-feet (16m) whale shark, is harmless to humans and feeds only on microscopic plankton.

Inevitably seafarers endowed the shark with supernatural abilities, particularly detection of blood at immense distances. This hyperbole has an underpinning of fact: in some species, more than 30 percent of the shark's brain is concerned with scent signals, and they can smell blood from half a mile (1km) away. Sharks are also attracted by spasmodic movement and a vertical posture in the water, both characteristics of dying fish. For this reason, swimmers are much more likely to be attacked when treading water than when actually swimming. In the sand sharks and mackerel sharks, even the embryos are fearsome. Initially, the pregnant females produce about a dozen foetuses, but as these grow they develop sharp teeth and start to eat each other, until there is only one left, whereupon it shifts in the oviduct so as to trigger its own birth. The zoologist who discovered this behaviour was attacked and bitten by a 9-inch (23cm) embryo while dissecting a dead female shark.

Traditional societies living near shark-infested waters show less hysterical, better informed attitudes than inlanders, but still call on supernatural powers for protection. In Sri Lanka, Brahman priests cast spells to stupefy sharks for the safety of pearl divers, and in New Zealand the hunting of the dog-shark is ritually controlled by Maori priests from the safety of the shore.

The power of the shark can be appropriated by gods. The Hindu god Vishnu is sometimes portrayed as emerging from the mouth of a monstrous shark. The Japanese storm god, "Shark-man", was a warrior who demonstrated his strength by swimming through the ocean with a shark under each arm.

SHARKS OF THE SOUTH SEAS

Coexisting with the shark inevitably bred attitudes of respect and reverence in many traditional societies. This is particularly so in the Pacific, where sharks are often worshipped as powerful shape-shifting spirits. In Fiji the most active deity was Dekuwaqa – chief god of both fishing and adultery – who took the form of a large basking shark that inhabited an underwater cave and guided the warriors' canoes on night raids. In the Trobriand Islands of Papua New Guinea young men set out alone in narrow canoes to "call" and catch a shark, the ultimate proof of manhood. The shark is called using a carved, propeller-shaped piece of light wood with a piece of fibrous rope attached via a hole in the middle. The other end of the rope forms a noose. The fisherman taps the wood on the surface of the water until a shark appears. Nobody is quite sure why sharks seem to come, as if hypnotized. When a shark starts circling the canoe, the fisherman lassoes it with the noose, drags it into the canoe and clubs it to death. If the shark is large, he may allow it to tire itself trying to drag the wooden float underwater before attempting to kill it.

A reliquary from the Solomon Islands. The carved shark opens up and the skull of the deceased is placed inside.

Crab, squid and octopus

Many shore crabs emerge to hunt only as the tide comes in, and retreat to burrows and crevices to escape the sight of predators as the tide recedes. Some scavenging species that search for washed-up detritus at low tide may evade predators by having internal clocks which allow them to emerge only when the low tide coincides with nightfall. The male fiddler crab must risk low tide in full daylight, because it uses an enlarged claw to signal to prospective mates. Whenever they appear, all crab species are clearly operating on a sophisticated biological clock, governed by the lunar tides. To the Incas of South America, the crab was an aspect of the Great Mother who devoured both time and the waning moon.

The crab's distinctive sideways movement has made it a widespread emblem (in China, for example) of human crookedness and unreliability. Its abandonment of its old shell (to allow for growth) and its habit of scuttling into and out of holes in the sand reinforce these associations. In medieval bestiaries the crab was the image of trickery and deceit: it was said to introduce a pebble into an oyster's opened shell, preventing it from closing again.

The Roman writer Pliny, whose gullibility is responsible for many spurious animal beliefs, records that the crab was supposedly a cure for snake bites, but was itself transformed into a venomous scorpion when the sun was in the constellation of Cancer. In Buddhist belief the crab is associated with the sleep of death, and the transitional period between incarnation and rebirth.

The octopus (like the crab) has been associated with the moon, the depths and the summer solstice. In myths of the classical world, the octopus was envisaged as a monster with foul breath: emerging from the sea onto dry land to eat, it would attack shipwrecked sailors by pulling them apart. The arms of an octopus have cuplike suckers on their inner surfaces. On the arms of squids and cuttlefish these are reinforced with horny rims, which are capable of cutting through flesh. To anyone attacked by one of these ani-

The octopus was a recurring motif in the art of the Minoan and Mycenaean civilizations in the Mediterranean, the coils of its eight arms making appealing swirls of decoration. It may appear with the spiral or swastika (symbol of the sun), and possibly had symbolic connections with thunder.

mals, it could quite easily have seemed that there were a number of biting mouths on each arm. Indeed, Greek vases in the Vatican museum which supposedly show the many-headed Hydra are clearly only slightly fanciful portraits of squids and octopuses.

Octopuses have eight equal-sized arms, or tentacles, and the largest octopus can measure 12 feet (3.5m) from tentacle-tip to tentacle-tip. Squids have eight short tentacles, and two that are much longer, which are used to catch prey. These longer tentacles are kept tucked under the body when not in use, but when they are stretched out, the giant squids of the genus *Architeuthis* can measure 50 feet (16m) in length. These giant squids are the inspiration for the sea monster called kraken.

The octopus is the most intelligent of invertebrates. It can change its colour, as well as the texture of its skin, when frightened or angry, or as camouflage when sneaking up on prey. Because of this habit (which was described by Aristotle and others) it was regarded as a symbol of inconstancy.

A panel from the Tempio Malatestiano in Rimini, showing the zodiacal sign of Cancer, created by the 15th-century artist Agostino di Duccio. In Greek myth, the crab gripped Herakles' heel in order to distract him while he was fighting the Hydra. The crab was crushed underfoot, but was set in the heavens by the goddess Hera, who hated Herakles.

LAND CONQUEST

Octopuses are complex and intelligent animals, and therefore more "advanced" than crabs. Yet the arthropods – creatures (including the crabs) with jointed legs, and bodies partially encased in jointed armour – were an evolutionary advance on the soft-bodied molluscs, among them the octopuses. The earliest fossil arthropods are trilobites, which survived between 220 and 570 million years ago.

The jointed armour that protected the arthropods in the sea also allowed them to spread to the land, by holding in moisture and preventing them from drying out. The first creatures to colonize the land were probably early crustaceans, the ancestors of the modern crabs, and arachnids, the ancestors of the scorpions. They emerged from the sea more than 400 million years ago. Crabs are remarkably adaptable, and there are species that live up trees, and even in deserts.

The horseshoe crab is a living fossil, most closely related to spiders, scorpions and the extinct trilobite. It has existed in its present form for at least 200 million years.

Imaginary Beasts

It is often possible to trace the evolution of a myth almost as surely as the evolution of a real animal. There are few imaginary beasts that do not contain some element of zoological truth. The early encounters of sailors with seals and sea-cows, explorers' accounts of equestrian tribes and great apes, and the discovery of fossils all fired the imaginations of storytellers to construct sirens, centaurs, Gorgons, Cyclopes, demons and dragons.

For example, it has been suggested that travellers' tales of the gorilla, filtering back to ancient Greece, were used by Homer to create the Cyclops (*Kuklops* means round-eye, not one-eye, and the gorilla has circular orbits in which the whites are barely visible). Ancient Athenian terracotta representations of a Gorgon show it having gorilla-like canine teeth, and legend describes the Gorgons as strangling leopards, which has long been a common story told about gorillas. Three probable gorilla skins on display in the temple of Melkart at Carthage, brought back from a voyage to West Africa in 525BC, were described by contemporary writers as *gorgadas*. Such early encounters, embellished by successions of poets, writers and credulous historians, helped create the menageries of inflated and composite monsters that still crowd the human imagination.

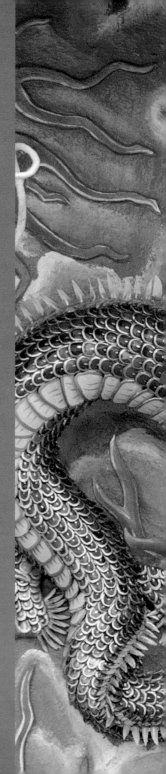

Dragons painted on the wall of Haw Par Villa in Singapore.

The Yeti and Big Foot

A recurring feature throughout the evolution of the human mind has been the imagining of animals that are in fact a magnification of the human body to superhuman size and power. Modern science has banished the unicorn and dragon to the realms of mythology but it has opened the floodgates to speculation about the existence of ancient bestial but humanoid creatures surviving in remote areas.

Ancient stories exist about the yeti – the Tibetan term for a Himalayan mountain spirit. However, the modern legend of the abominable snowman began in 1925 when an expedition photographer saw a strange man-like creature moving across the mountain slopes at an altitude of 15,000 feet (4,500m). It was soon lost to view but left behind footprints which were about 6 inches (15cm) long and 4 inches (10cm) wide, with five toes. Stories about the snowman were strengthened in 1951 when the climber Eric Shipton took photographs of a large footprint in the snow during his attempt on Mount Everest. A sherpa on the expedition claimed to have seen a yeti at a distance of only 75 feet (25m). He described it as "half man half beast, standing about 5 feet 6 inches [1.6m], with a tall pointed head, its body covered with reddish brown hair but with a hairless face".

Sightings of another superhuman creature called the alma have been reported from central Asia. One account describes it as being covered with reddish-brown hair and having a massive jaw and arms which reach below its knees. Local people have accused almas of raiding their farms. Some scientists believe that many of these humanoids, and almas in particular, could be remnants of Neanderthals who have survived in remote regions.

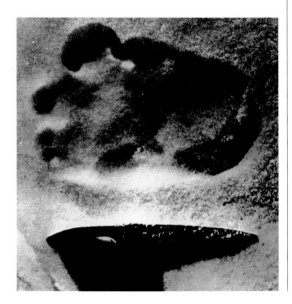

No plausible photographs exist of the yeti, but supposed footprints of the abominable snowman have been captured on film. This photograph was taken in 1958, and compares the size of the footprint with an axe-head. However, the photographic evidence is not conclusive as very large footprints are sometimes produced by mountain bears. When travelling at a lope, bears place their hindfeet partly over the imprints of the forefeet to produce tracks which look as if they were made by a large bipedal animal.

A painting of two yetis by a 20th-century sherpa. These images are based on the legend of the cannibal giant Metoh-kangmi, current throughout southern Tibet.

Until the 1950s it was widely believed that peculiar dome-shaped craniums found in the Himalayas were yeti scalps. On an expedition to the region in 1953, Sir Edmund Hillary discovered that they were in fact old goat-hair caps worn by the local inhabitants.

SASQUATCH

According to the Native Americans of the Pacific Northwest, a large population of strange animals used to inhabit Vancouver Island off the coast of British Columbia. Their name for this creature, Sasquatch, derived from folklore about a tribe of giants that used to inhabit the region.

There have been hundreds of modern sightings of Sasquatch, also widely known as Big Foot. Most have taken place on the mainland. Plaster casts have been made of what are claimed to be Big Foot footprints. One unusual piece of evidence appeared in 1967 when two monster seekers returned from northern California with a short clip of film which they claimed showed the elusive man-ape. The creature was more than 7 feet (2m) tall and lumbered across the camera's field of view. The film was poorly shot and zoologists who examined it were sceptical, many believing that it showed someone dressed in a monkey suit.

Centaur

The centaurs were descendants of Ixion, King of Thessaly, who had attempted to couple with the goddess Hera but had been fooled by a cloud Zeus had fashioned in her shape. This nebulous union produced Centaurus, who mated with wild mares, giving rise to a race of magical creatures, half human, half horse. The centaurs inhabited the wild Thessalonian countryside and were said to join the power and speed of the horse with the intelligence and emotion of humans.

Although centaurs could be wise and just, they were normally fierce and disruptive. Their sensuality associated them with the god Dionysus, and their strength and swiftness qualified them to be agents for the gods of the underworld. They were thus a common motif on funerary monuments.

A frieze c.500BC, from the Parthenon in Athens, showing a centaur trampling a Lapith. At the wedding of the King of the Lapiths, the centaurs tried to abduct his bride, leading to a battle, a detail of which is depicted here. Theseus helped the Lapiths to victory. It has been speculated that the myth of the centaur was born of early Greek encounters with mounted tribesmen.

Chiron was an exceptional centaur, the personification of wisdom and famous for his knowledge of archery, music and medicine. He tutored such archetypal Greek heroes as Achilles (seen here with Chiron in a 2,000-year-old Roman wall-painting) and Jason and imparted his knowledge of medicine to Asclepius, the master physician. Zeus awarded him recognition as the zodiacal constellation Sagittarius.

Minotaur

The invention of the Minotaur – the half-man, half-bull creature of Greek mythology – may have been influenced by earlier imagery of the bull-leaping cult of Minoan Crete. The Greek myth tells a tale of divine retribution, unnatural sexuality and human inventiveness.

The story relates how the legendary King Minos of Crete prayed for a bull to sacrifice to Poseidon. However, the bull that appeared was so magnificent that he decided to keep it for himself and the god punished him by making his wife Pasiphaë fall obsessively in love with the beast. Hiding inside a hollow model of a heifer, made for her by Daedalus the master craftsman, she coupled with the bull and subsequently gave birth to the Minotaur. Minos was furious and ordered Daedalus to build an underground labyrinth to imprison the hybrid monster.

Trapped in the labyrinth, the Minotaur was fed on sacrificial children sent annually from Athens as tribute until Theseus volunteered to kill the monster (shown here on a 2,500-year-old Athenian plate). Ariadne, the daughter of Minos, gave him a ball of twine by which he retraced his steps after slaying the Minotaur.

The myth of Theseus and the Minotaur is rich in meaning. The bull-man represents nature's unbridled passions which must be securely locked away but periodically placated. The labyrinth is sometimes interpreted as a metaphor for the tortuous path of life, and the length of twine that leads out of the labyrinth is understood to be the spark of divine instinct which unerringly illuminates the right path. The wistful Minotaur shown in this 1880 painting by George Frederick Watts demonstrates the Victorian sentimentalization of nature.

Sphinx

The sphinx is one of the most enduring and evocative of the ancient world's imaginary creatures. Over the millennia, it has also been one of the most mutable. Sometimes it has been male, sometimes female. It has been variously depicted as a lion, a leopard, a cheetah or a tiger, sometimes with wings and sometimes without. In medieval Europe, as travellers' tales of apes, monkeys and exotic peoples became hopelessly tangled together, the sphinx came to have a monkey's body. This protean character is appropriate, because the sphinx's origins lie far back in the past, among shamanic cultures which almost certainly believed that there were some humans who could change and mix their forms with those of animals.

Associations with strength, spiritual protection and the cycle of life and death are recurring features of sphinx symbolism. In Egypt, where religious beliefs surrounded domestic cats, lions and leopards, the sphinx usually took the form of a man's head on a lion's body. The mythical creature emphasized the status of the pharaoh as omniscient and omnipotent divine ruler.

Affected equally by Near Eastern and Egyptian ideas, the sphinx appeared in the Greek world around 1600BC in a winged form with a woman's head, a lion's body and the wings of an eagle. It was depicted with a flat cap on its head with a flame-like projection on top. Later it was adorned with a long-tiered wig. The Greek sphinx was most famous in the classical world for its role in the tragedy of Oedipus. In Greek mythology the sphinx was also seen as a spiritual protector. As such it was a decorative motif on the helmet of Athena, the warrior-goddess of Athens, and a frequent image on gravestones.

The sphinx was transformed from an image of evil into one of erotic fascination in this late-19th-century painting by F. Khnopff. Classical in style, the painting blends the ancient imagery of shape-shifting beliefs with modern attitudes toward ambivalent sexuality.

THE GREEK RIDDLE

Sent as a curse by Hera, queen of the Olympian gods, the woman-headed sphinx terrorized ancient Thebes by killing anyone who failed to answer her riddle. Confronted by the demon during his wanderings, Oedipus was asked: "What has four legs in the morning, two legs at midday, and three legs in the evening ?" He answered correctly "Man", who crawls in infancy, walks upright in maturity, and uses a stick in old age. The sphinx was so enraged at having her riddle answered that she threw herself into the sea, and Oedipus was hailed as the city's saviour.

A Greek kylix, or shallow cup, made in 470 BC, showing Oedipus and the sphinx.

BELOW RIGHT *This alabaster figure from Memphis in Egypt is typical of ancient Egyptian sphinxes, the most famous of which is at Giza where the recumbent, lion-bodied statue of the pharaoh Khafre (c.2575–2465 BC) stands as a guardian to his tomb. The tradition of the sphinx as royal portrait persisted throughout ancient Egyptian history, combining the idea of the lion, the king of beasts, with that of the divine ruler to symbolize the union of intellectual and physical powers incarnate in the pharaoh.*

Chimera and griffin

Explosive natural gas flaring out from cracks in the rocks on the mountains of Lycia in southwest Turkey probably inspired one of the most celebrated hybrids of Greek myth, the Chimera. This fire-breathing lion, which had a horn-tossing goat as its midriff and a serpent's tail, symbolized the many destructive natural forces that seemed beyond human control – and could be conquered only with supernatural assistance. In Greek myth, such assistance was provided by the miraculous flying horse, Pegasus, which carried the hero Bellerophon above the monster's open jaws. From this position, Bellerophon was able to drop lead down the Chimera's throat, which melted in its fiery breath and choked it.

The griffin, griffon or gryphon emerged as a formidable image of power in the art of ancient west Asia, combining a lion's body with the head, breast, wings and claws of an eagle. These two creatures were symbolic rulers of earth and air respectively. To the ancient Hebrews, the griffin represented Persia with its dualistic religion of Zoroastrianism. It was a Graeco-Roman emblem of the solar god Apollo, as well as being associated with Athene, the goddess of wisdom, and the avenging goddess, Nemesis. Vengeance and persecution were also its early Christian symbolism, but in medieval art it came to represent the dual human/divine nature of Christ.

Like other forceful hybrids, the griffin was also a guardian figure, especially in Minoan Crete, where it represented vigilant courage. The ancient Greeks believed that griffins guarded hoards of gold in Scythia and India, and the historian Herodotus, in the 5th century BC, described them as building their nests out of gold.

This bronze Etruscan sculpture is the classic image of the Chimera; it captures the power and violence that the ancients sought to embody in animal hybrids. Called the Chimera d'Arezzo, it shows a creature apparently ready to devour even itself. Its mother, Echidna, a hybrid of nymph and snake, was blamed for giving birth to many other monsters of Greek myth, including the three-headed dog Cerberus and the Hydra.

Unicorn

Different types of unicorn occur in legends worldwide. The Chinese unicorn is a dragon with a stag's head bearing only one antler. The *unicornis* of the Romans was, from contemporary accounts, clearly a rhinoceros. The Greek physician, Ctesias, in a 4th-century BC history of Persia and Assyria, was the first to describe a unicorn as being equine, "a kind of wild ass, white with a dark red head and an 18-inch [45cm] horn on its forehead which, when ground to powder, yields a certain remedy against epilepsy and the most potent poison".

His account clearly combines three animals: the onager, a ferocious wild ass of western Asia; the blackbuck, a species of antelope in which one horn of the male sometimes atrophies; and the Indian rhinoceros, whose powdered horn the Chinese used as a form of medicine. Nevertheless, from Ctesias' description the unicorn evolved into the most graceful and poetic of all mythical creatures.

Fossilized mammoth tusks discovered in the early Middle Ages were often claimed to be unicorn horns, and sold as panaceas. The unicorn was not commonly depicted with the now-familiar spiral horn until after the 15th century, when crooked apothecaries discovered the vast profits to be made from selling the twisted ivory tusk of the narwhal (a kind of porpoise) as the horn of the unicorn.

This detail from the 15th-century French tapestry The Lady of the Unicorn *refers to medieval courtly allegories of chaste love taming animal desires. A link between virginity and the unicorn goes back to a Graeco-Roman tradition associating the creature with Artemis and Diana. Christianity adapted this tradition by modifying the image of the fierce unicorn until it became a symbol of the Immaculate Conception, and its horn a form of spiritual penetration.*

Pegasus

In Greek mythology, the winged stallion Pegasus sprang from the blood of Medusa when she was beheaded by Perseus. A lunar animal, Pegasus was usually depicted as white (the colour of the moon) with golden wings, and wherever he stamped his crescent-shaped hooves on the ground a fountain would spring forth. This was reflected in the stallion's Greek name, Hippocrene, which comes from *hippos* (horse) and *krene* (fountain), and in the fact that Pegasus came to symbolize the poetic side of human nature. Anyone who drank from one of Pegasus' fountains was believed to gain poetic inspiration from its waters.

The only person ever to tame Pegasus was the hero Bellerophon, who used the stallion to reach the Chimera's lair. He later offended Zeus by trying to ride Pegasus to Olympus: the god unseated him and then turned Pegasus into a constellation.

The classical image of Pegasus is shown in these terracotta horses, which were made in the 6th–5th century BC and come from the Temple of Tarquinia in Italy. They include the magical bridle which in the Greek myth was a present from the goddess of wisdom, Athena, to Bellerophon. The hero threw it over the head of Pegasus, which was the only way to tame the unruly beast.

Shown here in an 18th-century painting by Giovanni Battista, Bellerophon flew on Pegasus to the Chimera's hideout. Bellerophon was sent to kill the fire-breathing Chimera as one of the supposedly impossible tasks set for him by King Isolates. As the offspring of Poseidon's alliance with Medusa, Pegasus was a relative of the Chimera.

Phoenix

The phoenix of classical myth was a bird of gorgeous plumage which inhabited the Arabian desert. Every few hundred years it would smear its wings with myrrh and burst into flames, only to rejunvenate itself from the ashes of the fire to live anew.

The myth of the phoenix came to symbolize resurrection and life after death in many different cultures. The Egyptians regarded this fabulous bird as an emblem of the sun god Ra: it resembled an eagle in size and shape. To the Romans it was seen as a symbol of enduring empire. In China it is associated with the sun and moon and encapsulates the union of yin and yang; and when depicted next to the dragon (see pp.154–5) it represents the undivided nature of imperial power.

The phoenix was used by Christianity as an expression of faith. In rising from the flames, the bird symbolized the triumph of the faithful over death.

In the Christian tradition it was said that of all the creatures in the Garden of Eden only the phoenix did not eat of the forbidden fruit. It became identified with Christ threatened by the fires of passion, but resurrected by the grace of God.

The magical form of the phoenix in Chinese art, pictured here among peonies and rocks in a 17th-century tapestry, symbolized the elements of the universe: its cock's head was the sun, its swallow's back the crescent moon, its tail the trees and flowers, its feet the earth, and its fiery wings the wind.

Dragon

there is a description of the terrible Leviathan: "Out of his mouth go burning lamps, and sparks of fire leap out." This may be one of the earliest descriptions of the dragon as breathing fire. Christianity also adopted the dragon's association with evil, and viewed the fire-breathing beast as a symbol of desolation and death, and thus an image of Satan. Dragons were metaphorical barriers to enlightenment, and as such fought terrible battles with Christian saints. These were echoes of myths from all over the world of gods and heroes, such as Horus, Marduk and Thor, who had to fight dragons to win order from chaos.

One origin of the dragon's dual role as primeval master of the land and the sacred waters can be found in Herodotus' description of the monster from the 5th century BC. "It inhabits the land and the water, lays and hatches its eggs on the former and spends most of its day there, but passes the night in the water ... Its claws are strong, the scaly skin on its back cannot be sundered. In Egypt it is called *champsa*, but the Ionians call it *krokodil*." The Egyptians treated crocodiles as sacred beasts. They fed them and tamed them to the point where they could be touched. According to Herodotus they hung "golden rings with cut stones" in a crocodile's earholes, and "decked out its paws with golden bracelets", a practice which is probably the origin of legends about the dragon's hoard of gold.

Semitic peoples often demonized the sacred animals of the Egyptians who persecuted them. In the Book of Job

The dragon in Britain blends Celtic and Christian belief. It once represented royalty and was an emblem of war for King Arthur, whose father was Uther Pendragon or "chief dragon". The dragon is still a national emblem of Wales, recalling its Celtic past. In England, St George (above, in a 16th-century English church window) became patron saint for his legendary slaughter of a fearsome dragon.

In Greek mythology the dragon was often portrayed as the legless python. It was an obstacle to wealth and knowledge, and was the guardian of secret things and places, such as the Golden Fleece. (In Greek the word *dragon* is related to *drakos*, meaning to see or to watch.)

In China the dragon or *lung* had a positive and more sophisticated role. Chinese beliefs held the dragon to be a symbol of supreme spirituality and the image of the divine power of transformation. It represented yang, the principle of heaven, activity and maleness, and was the emblem of the imperial family.

RIGHT *A dragon dating from 570BC and made out of coloured ceramic bricks, from the gates of Ishtar at Babylon. In Babylonian mythology the creation of the civilized world was achieved only when the hero Marduk slew Tiamat, the mother of the gods, who appeared as a monstrous she-dragon. Marduk split Tiamat's carcass into two halves, one half making the sky and the other the earth's surface. The combat between Marduk and Tiamat was ritually re-enacted in Babylon each year.*

THE CHINESE DRAGON

According to Chinese lore the dragon is the first of the Four Auspicious Animals or animals of good omen. Through five of its major manifestations it influences many aspects of life: as the Celestial Dragon it is protector of the heavenly abodes of the gods; as the Imperial Dragon (pictured above in embroidered silk) it symbolizes both the rain and the rising sun; as "Mang" it signifies temporal power; as "Li" it is the hornless one which controls the sea and represents the depths of scholarly wisdom; and as "Chiao" it inhabits the mountaintops and represents the statesman.

Sea monster

In the Mesopotamian creation myth, the mighty ocean was the monster Tiamat, the turbulent chaos which must be subdued in order to achieve an ordered world. Leviathan, the Hebrew version of Tiamat, was a monster of the deep rather than the deep itself, which Jahweh alone could dominate.

Despite these and other ancient accounts, the real popularity of sea monster stories can be traced to increased marine exploration in the 15th and 16th centuries, and to one book in particular. *A Concise History of the Goths, Swedes and Wends, and Other Northern Peoples*, published in 1555 by

Andromeda's mother boasted that her daughter was lovelier than the Nereids, or sea-nymphs. The Nereids turned to Poseidon, god of the sea, for revenge, and he conjured up a sea monster to terrorize the coast. To appease the monster, Andromeda's father King Cepheus prepared to sacrifice her but she was rescued by Perseus, as shown in this painting from 1554–6 by Titian.

an ex-bishop of Upsala, Olaus Magnus, contains pictures and descriptions of most of the monsters that were to enter folklore. The kraken, of Scandinavian myth, was based on a giant octopus or squid and was said to be able to entangle huge ships in its tentacles and drag them into the deep. Sperm whales, walruses and elephant seals all entered Magnus' book in fantastical shapes. Dugongs, or sea-cows, whose skin is often flesh-pink in colour, appeared as mermaids, supposedly feminine down to their fishy tails. Their close cousins from antiquity, the Sirens, originated in Egypt as half-woman, half-bird creatures. However, in Greek myth, when they lost a musical duel with the Muses, they changed their bird features for fishes' tails and migrated to the shore to sing seafarers to their doom.

Monster stories were also fuelled by grotesque deep-sea species, such as angler fish, black swallowers and gulper eels, which appeared in fishermen's nets and were made all the more hideous by having burst on the way to the surface because of the decrease in pressure. Other monsters were based on fossils. The first reliably described *ichthyosaur*, a porpoise-like reptile that died out more than 66 million years ago, occurs in a book from 1669 by the Englishman Edward Lhuyd. He thought it was a sea-dragon, not flesh and blood at all, but made of stone.

A 17th-century tiled panel featuring a sea monster shaped like a griffin, from Palacio de los Fronteira in Portugal. Many terrestrial monsters had their marine counterparts. In the Middle Ages, this symmetry was maintained among real beasts too. The walrus was assumed by the medieval historian Albertus Magnus to be a "whale-elephant", and Olaus Magnus described it as a "monstrous swine".

LOCH NESS MONSTER

The Loch Ness monster was first mentioned in an account of the life of the 6th-century Saint Columba, but the modern legend began in 1933 when the owners of an inn close to the Scottish loch reportedly saw a huge animal with a slender neck, small head and humped back ploughing through its deep waters. The most famous photograph of the Loch Ness monster (right) was taken in 1934 by a London surgeon, who admitted in his will some 60 years later that it had been a fake.

However, the legend persists, and teams of British, American and Japanese scientists conduct research periodically at the loch. Despite hi-tech equipment, including sonar and computerized image enhancement, the gloom in the depths of the loch, which plunges to more than 900 feet (277m), makes thorough investigation impossible. One theory is that the creature is

one of a remnant family of *plesiosaurs*, survivors from the age of dinosaurs, which fossil evidence suggests became extinct about 70 million years ago.

Werewolf

Tales of were-animals (from the Old English word for man, "wer") exist around the world. The idea of humans shape-shifting into fierce predatory beasts finds expression in the leopard-men and hyena-men of Africa, or the were-jaguars of the Amazon. In Europe and much of Asia, wolves have been the most feared animals for most of human history, and it is no coincidence that werewolf scares are most common in areas where real wolves still hunt. In the fierce winter of 1968 in the highlands of Iran, snowstorms forced wolves down from the mountains to the valleys where they attacked and devoured eighteen people, giving rise to renewed fears of werewolves.

The Greek origins of the werewolf legend lay in Arcadia, a mountainous region of the Peloponnese, which was overrun with wolves. Devotees of the cult of Lycaean Zeus ("Wolf-Zeus") gathered once a year and ate a mixture of human flesh and ordinary meat prepared by priests. Anyone who tasted the human flesh turned into a werewolf.

Porphyria, a metabolic disorder that

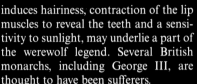

The full moon is associated with madness (lunacy) and the transformation of werewolves.

induces hairiness, contraction of the lip muscles to reveal the teeth and a sensitivity to sunlight, may underlie a part of the werewolf legend. Several British monarchs, including George III, are thought to have been sufferers.

Tales of feral children, raised by wolves, have existed since the Romans. A notorious recent case is the wolf-girls of Midnapore, in India, who were found in 1920. However, their wolf-like characteristics, including a heightened sense of smell and hearing, a preference for raw meat and the habit of lapping up fluids with their tongues are all symptoms that can be found in abused, autistic children. As the psychoanalyst Bruno Bettelheim said of feral children, their behaviour "seems to be the result of some person's – usually their parents' – inhumanity and not the result, as it was assumed, of animals' – particularly wolves' – humanity."

A woodcut from Nuremberg, c.1683, illustrating the contemporary story of a man who was executed, and whose unquiet spirit took over a wolf and terrorized the district. In the Middle Ages, and in parts of Europe for a long time afterward, the souls of the executed were thought to return as werewolves or vampires, so gibbets were often found at crossroads to confuse and entrap them.

THE WEREWOLF AS CANNIBAL

In late medieval Europe, social and religious intolerance manifested itself in both the witch-burning craze and a renewed belief in werewolves. Wolves were common and posed a real threat to livestock and people, but mass hysteria and religious frenzy played a crucial role in spreading alarm. Contemporary accounts describe the werewolf variously as a giant human with a wolf's head and feet, or as a huge wolf which walked on hind legs like a man. Werewolves were also confused with unkempt "wild men", as in the above woodcut of a "Cannibal, or Werewolf", by the German artist Cranach the Elder, made in 1510–15.

Selective Gazetteer

Africa and Arabia

Animals loom larger in ancient Egyptian thought than in that of any other religion, at any other time. Even the lowly dung beetle, which rolls balls of dung both to feed itself and to lay its eggs in, became a symbol of rebirth, as the scarab that rolls the sun into the sky each day. Whether consciously or not, the Egyptians were recognizing the vital role the dung beetle plays in disseminating seeds, fertilizing the soil and ensuring the constant recycling of elements that makes life possible. Not all animals were so revered, however.

The camel was first domesticated in central Arabia between 3,000 and 6,000 years ago, yet there is no camel-headed god in the animalistic Egyptian pantheon, nor is there any word for camel in the language of ancient Egypt. It was once thought that this was because the camel was too lowly a beast of burden to merit godhood, but the cat – originally valued only as a ratcatcher – was worshipped, and even if the camel was never a god, one would certainly expect some reference to it. In fact, however, the ancient Egyptian civilization was tied to the Nile valley – a fertile area with plentiful vegetation – and the camel has not only adapted well to a life in the desert, it is actually uncomfortable in richer surroundings, and becomes prone to disease. Also, the camel's odour is unpleasant, and sometimes even frightening, to other animals, a fact exploited by the early Persians in battle to rout their opponents' cavalry. For these reasons the ancient Egyptians had very little to do with camels. It was only when the whole of Arabia and northern Africa became more arid and desertified, during the later days of the Roman Empire, that the camel became a valued beast of burden.

Camels are suited to a desert environment in many ways. They can drink a third of their body weight in one session. Most mammals have to keep a fairly constant body temperature or they will get a fever, and one way to keep the body's temperature constant in hot climates is to sweat. Camels can conserve water by allowing their body temperature to fluctuate by up to 6°C, and they also have an efficient excretory system that results in highly concentrated urine and powder-dry feces (an added bonus to their owners – dry dung burns more easily as fuel). As a result, camels can travel 300 miles (500km) across burning desert between watering holes, their flat, splayed feet allowing them to walk on shifting sand without sinking. They are still an essential part of the lives of

The camels include the two-humped Bactrian camel of Asia and the one-humped dromedary of Arabia, as well as the llama, alpaca, vicuna and guanaco of the New World. The llama (a pack animal) and alpaca (a wool provider) were economically vital to the Aztec Empire. Some 90 percent of the 14 million camels in the world are dromedaries.

nomadic desert peoples. In Islamic Arabia, where the smuggling of alcohol is a large part of a thriving black market, camels are valued as "one case", "two case" or "three case" animals, according to how much whiskey they can carry.

Colonial powers

There is a recurring pattern in Africa of new human arrivals depriving indigenous populations of their traditional rights and relationships to animals. The Bushmen occupied much of southern Africa for thousands of years before the cattle-owning Bantu came down from the north c.10AD. To the hunter-gatherer Bushmen, a cow was just another animal to be killed when they were hungry. The Bantu would not tolerate this, and slowly, over the course of 800 years, drove the Bushmen into the wilderness of the Kalahari desert.

The pattern was almost exactly repeated when Europeans began colonizing the region in the 19th century. Peoples such as the Basotho lived under the *mafisa* tradition, where the king owned all the tribe's cattle, which he loaned to his followers for them to use. Cattle raiding was an accepted part of this way of life, and a chief could not punish his followers for it. To the European settlers, people who practised *mafisa* were cattle thieves, to be chased off or annihilated.

Southern Africans sold ivory to the wealthy Shona of eastern Zimbabwe from at least the 14th century. Further north, the tribes of West Africa wiped out their elephant populations by trading tusks with the Arabs from the 17th century. The 19th- and 20th-century white colonial powers decided that they owned all the resources of their colonies, including the game. Tribesmen who hunted were now hunted in their turn, as poachers, while game departments sold white hunters the right to kill. A "sportsman" had to buy licenses to hunt game, including a special one for elephant, the final cost of which depended on the weight of ivory in the tusks.

Following the CITES (Convention on International Trade in Endangered Species) meeting in Washington in 1973, pressure grew to ban all trade in ivory worldwide. Some African countries saw this as a continuation of white governments telling them what to do. Zimbabwe and Botswana have been successful at conserving their elephant populations by encouraging hunting as part of a programme of culling, and using the revenue to fund the fight against poachers. Curiously, they argue that the old colonial system of charging a hunter according to the weight of ivory on the kill is conservationally sound. The hunters want big tuskers because they make the best trophies. The government wants the hunters to kill big tuskers because that way they make more money. The big tuskers are usually old, dominant bulls, which are stopping younger, more fertile males from breeding, so the herd as a whole also benefits.

Because of the Bushmen's precarious relationship with the environment, their population never grew very large, and was always scattered, so they were unable to put up an organized resistance to the pastoralist Bantu. However, their hunting skills made them formidable guerilla fighters, and they were sometimes hired as mercenaries in disputes between Bantu tribes.

The Masai Mara game reserve in Kenya is famous for its prides of black-maned lions, some of which number up to 40 animals. Traditionally, a Masai boy must spear a lion in order to become a man, and although the practice is illegal a handful of ambitious Masai youths are still gored, sometimes fatally, each year.

Europe

There are far fewer animal species in the forests of Europe than there are at comparable latitudes in the forests of North America. The reasons for this are numerous. European countryside has a much longer history of management – there is only one genuinely wild, primeval forest in the whole of the continent: Bialowieza on the Poland-Belarus border. In many parts of Europe, predatory species, as well as the larger grazing animals, were long ago hunted to extinction. Wolves were exterminated in England in 1281, although they lasted longer in Scotland, and the last wolf in Ireland was killed some time around 1709.

There were fewer species in Europe even before the intervention of humankind, however, because many more European than American species were wiped out whenever there was an ice age. The conditions during the ice ages were no more severe in Europe: the scale of the extinctions was so much greater simply because the major European mountain ranges, such as the Alps and the Pyrenees, stretch east to west, whereas the American mountain ranges, such as the Rockies and the Appalachians, stretch north to south. This meant that, as the glaciers and ice sheets advanced, American species could migrate south before them, and survive, while European species found themselves blockaded by unpassable mountains, and perished.

City life
The industrial revolution began in Europe, and increasing urbanization has been one of the most profound influences on the structure and behaviour of animal populations. With the growth of the cities and the shrinking of feeding opportunities in the countryside, red foxes have become predominantly an urban species in much of Europe. Similarly, the brown or Norwegian rat (which actually originated in Asia) has since the Roman Empire found sewers and drains a perfect substitute for its natural habitat of holes in riverbanks.

The typical European city-dweller has always been blind to much of the surrounding urban wildlife. Instead, European cities imported animals from further afield and invented the modern "zoo", a word deriving from the collection of the Zoological Society of London, which was set up in the early 19th century. Even London Zoo, however, was optimistically intended as a force for technological progress, and part of the drive for ever-increasing human control over nature. The goal of its founders was the "introducing and domesticating of new Breeds or Varieties of Animals ... useful in Common Life", a dream whose consummation was the spread of the grey squirrel and the golden hamster.

The pigeons common in cities throughout Europe evolved from rock doves. Like many birds that originally lived on sheer cliff faces, pigeons have adapted well to the walls, ledges and window-sills of typical tall city buildings. In addition to thriving as urban wildlife, pigeons have been tamed and used to carry messages. In many European countries, most notably Belgium, pigeon racing is a sport that attracts thousands of participants.

China

The relationship of the Chinese with the animal world has often been one of intense practicality, mistaken by observers as mysticism or superstition. According to the sacred *Book of Songs*, the first zoo in China was Wu-Wang's "Park of Intelligence", built in 1050BC, in which he kept tigers, deer, rhinoceroses "and other great beasts". As well as entertaining the emperor, the park provided a constant stock of rare and exotic animals to send as gifts to friendly princes. This tradition persisted, and in 685AD the imperial Japanese accounts describe a gift of two white bears and 70 white bear skins sent to the *tenno* of Japan by the Chinese emperor. It was assumed by naturalists that these were polar bears, although a Chinese chronicle from 621BC mentions the white bears as coming from the bamboo forests of Yunnan province, and describes them as having black markings. It was not until 1869 that Père Armand David rediscovered the giant panda in the hills of Szechuan.

The panda remained a tool of foreign policy into the 1960s and 1970s era of "Panda Diplomacy", when the Communist government made gifts of "breeding pairs" to favoured countries. Pandas are extremely reluctant to mate, and such pairs never reproduced. Western zoos undertook swapping programmes to bring together animals that might be compatible, but with little success. In 1994, London Zoo's last panda, Ming Ming, was returned to China.

Animal observation
The Chinese style of wrestling, *shuai-chiao*, has its origins in an ancient game called *chiao-ti*, in which contestants strapped cow-horns to their heads and butted each other. Shaolin Temple Boxing, popularly known as Kung Fu, was supposedly invented by Bodhidarma, the First Patriarch of Zen Buddhism, around 500AD. Most of the surviving Shaolin styles were invented by monks, and based on the movements of animals. They include Praying Mantis Style, White Crane Style and Tiger Claw Style. The martial art known as Tai-chi-chuan is said to have been created by the Taoist recluse Chang San-feng, after he saw how a snake's sinuous movements eluded the stabbing beak of a crane.

Government-legislated observation of animals saved millions of lives in the 20th century under Mao. People in earthquake-prone areas had to report restive behaviour on the part of their family pets, as well as noting when the water levels in their wells dropped – both traditional warnings of earthquakes. In fact, cats are sensitive to electrical potentials that build up before quakes, and this "primitive" early-warning system proved remarkably effective.

Early Chinese chronicles record the existence of "snow monkeys" found at altitudes of up to 10,000 feet (3,000m). Just like the stories of pandas and tapirs, which subsequently proved to be true, these reports were discounted by Westerners until, in 1870, Père David acquired the skin of a colourful, snub-nosed monkey from the mountains of the Tibetan border. The macaque monkeys that live in the mountains of northern Japan have learned to sit out especially cold weather in the natural hot baths of volcanic springs.

India

The most reverential attitudes toward animals are to be found in India. They can be traced to the 7,000-year-old Hindu belief – reinforced by Buddhism – in the cycle of birth and rebirth of the soul, which may manifest its earthly form in animals as well as humans. The 330 million gods of Hinduism are all aspects of one god, yet each aspect has its own community or region that pays it special homage, and its own form, which is often that of an animal. In the Rajasthani town of Deshnok there is a 16th-century temple to the goddess Karniji, who is symbolically related to rats. It swarms with a population of 10,000 real rats, which have given up their elusive nocturnal habits and come out in daylight to share food brought by pilgrims, often eating from the same plate. Even at the height of the rat-transmitted plague scare that gripped India in 1994, these animals were not harmed or persecuted in any way. Monkeys live in temples throughout India, surviving on the offerings brought for them by worshippers of the monkey god Hanuman. Cows are even more widely revered, an attitude that probably arrived in India with nomads from the north who, like the Masai of Africa, regarded their cows as markers of their wealth, and would not contemplate harming them.

Beasts of burden
The elephant's proverbial memory is a fact. Elephants are reluctant to breed in captivity, their gestation period is nearly two years, and they spend a great deal of time looking after their young: therefore most of the working elephants that are still used in India are taken from the wild. Originally, as with most animals, captured elephants were trained through cruelty. There are numerous well documented cases of docile elephants, more than 30 years after their training, crushing to death someone in a crowd who subsequently turned out to have been their trainer. Since at least the 14th century, therefore, a newly caught elephant has been trained by having a man in a colourful disguise starve and abuse it, only to be driven away by the man who will eventually be its partner, or *mahout*. The *mahout* pampers the animal, and feeds it, and after two or three weeks of this sort of brainwashing the elephant has formed a lifelong attitude of affection and obedience toward its new handler.

The elephant is not a conspicuously successful pack animal, as Hannibal and countless other generals discovered. Despite its great bulk, the most it can carry is some 600lb (270kg), or about the same as eight foot soldiers. Its main use as a working animal lies in hauling timber: an adult Indian elephant can drag a weight of more than two tons.

Indian elephants are smaller and lighter than their African counterparts, with domed foreheads and more sloping backs. Both species have been used in warfare. The elephants Hannibal took across the Alps to try to conquer Rome were African. The elephants Darius III of Persia used unsuccessfully against Alexander at Issus were Indian. When the two species were pitted against each other at the Battle of Raphia in 217BC, despite their greater size the African elephants of Ptolemy turned and ran before the Indian elephants of Antiochus. After this, the African elephant gradually acquired a reputation as being impossible to train, which it retained into the 20th century.

Australia and the Pacific

When the *Victoria*, the last surviving vessel of Magellan's fleet and the first ship to sail around the world, put into Seville harbour in 1522, its cargo contained some brightly coloured bird skins presented to the captain by the Sultan of Batjan, an island in the Moluccas. The Sultan claimed that they had originally come from one of the islands surrounding the fabled southern continent. The first naturalists to examine the skins had no idea that they had been skilfully prepared and dried. Noting the birds' long, banner-like feathers and their lack of flesh and bones, or even feet, scholars concluded that these were "higher beings, free from the necessity of other creatures to touch the ground". They were weightless and "undecaying". In this way the legend of the "bird of paradise" was born. It proved a tenacious myth: even the great 18th-century naturalist Linnaeus called the creature *Paradisea apoda*, the footless bird of paradise.

Perhaps uniquely in the history of rare and sought-after species, the early European quest for birds of paradise produced more human corpses than it did trophies. After the discovery that the birds came from New Guinea, armies of 19th-century naturalists and animal collectors lost their lives to disease or head-hunters while in pursuit of specimens. Alfred Russel Wallace was the first man to bring living birds to Europe, in 1862. His researches gave the final impetus to Charles Darwin's book *The Descent of Man and Sexual Selection*. In 1884, an ornithologist called Otto Finsch became so obsessed with birds of paradise that he raised the German flag in northeastern New Guinea, signalling the start of the real slaughter. The German New Guinea Company, discovering that the island had no other exploitable resources, decided to make all it could out of the birds. Some 5,000 were shot in the first five years of colonization, and sold to the fashion industry to decorate hats.

Island hopping

Shortly after its discovery, New Zealand was nicknamed by zoologists *Ornithogaea*, the continent of birds. This was not because it contained more species than anywhere else, but because birds were the highest form of life to have evolved on the island. Because they did not have to take to the air to escape predators or build nests in trees, out of the reach of rodents, the birds of New Zealand gradually lost the power of flight. As a result, they were largely defenceless when the the Polynesians of Raiatea arrived in the 14th century. The dogs and the stowaway rats brought in Polynesian canoes decimated the earthbound birds. Many species, including a flightless bird of prey and a giant duck, became extinct with-

There are nearly 40 species of birds of paradise in New Guinea. They are closely related to crows and ravens, and Darwin used their diversity and brilliance to support his theories of natural selection. The males are exotic, and compete to attract the attention of the dowdy females. It is the female that chooses which she breeds with. By choosing the gaudiest male, she is more likely to have gaudy male offspring, which in turn will tend to be chosen by other females. In this way she increases her chances of passing on her genes, via her male offspring. At the same time, the species as a whole becomes more and more exotic.

in a few years. Others, such as the nocturnal flightless parrot, the kakapo, retreated to remote parts of the island. By 1990 the kakapo, which can reach 8lb (3.5kg) and live for 60 years, had been reduced to a breeding population of less than 50. The takahe, a large flightless marsh bird long thought to be extinct, was rediscovered only in 1948, and survives in small numbers on the South Island.

An isolated island will tend to evolve highly specialized species that naturally have no defences to creatures they have never encountered. There may be no predators for the larger animals, so they will not even run away when threatened. Between the 17th and 19th centuries, European ships took some 200,000 unresisting giant tortoises from the Galapagos to use as food on their voyages. Yet the same isolation often means that introduced species can diversify into new ecological niches in ways that would not be possible on the more competitive mainland. The 42 species of Hawaiian honeycreeper have vastly different bills and feeding habits. The bright red iiwi has a long, curving bill and a tongue that can be curled into a tube, for nectar-feeding. The anianiau has a short beak and a fringed tongue to trap insects. Others are adapted to eat various different fruits or seeds. Yet they have all adaptively radiated out from one ancestral species of warbler, probably brought to the island by humans as a pet.

Living fossils
Australia has suffered two main waves of invasion by alien species. The first was when the prehistoric ancestors of the Aboriginals came south from Java with their dogs, or dingoes. The second was when Europeans brought cattle and rabbits. The cattle brought another alien species in their wake, when it transpired that the local dung beetles – which had evolved alongside kangaroos – were not strong enough to roll cow droppings. Without the beetles, the cattle dung was not decomposing, and so African dung beetles had to be imported if the plains were not, literally, to become knee-deep in droppings.

Some native carnivores, including marsupial lions and bears, could not compete with dingoes. Many more, such as the Tasmanian wolf, were eventually exterminated by cattle ranchers. The strangest of Australia's creatures, the platypus, survived. The platypus caused controversy from the moment it was discovered in 1799. It was claimed by some to be a link between reptiles and mammals – like reptiles, it lays soft-shelled eggs. Others thought it a missing link between mammals and birds – it has a bill, and webbed feet. Others thought it a degenerate marsupial – it has a pouch. In fact it is a monotreme, a distinct class of mammal. Although the female has no nipples, she possesses glands that leak milk into the fur, which is then licked up by her young.

Except for the opossum of the Americas, marsupials – animals which have no placenta, so that their foetuses develop in a pouch – are found only in Australasia. The largest surviving marsupial is the kangaroo. Superbly adapted for its life in open country, the kangaroo moves in rapid bounds, using its long tail for balance. The absence of monkeys in the jungles of New Guinea has led to the evolution of tree kangaroos which, unlike their Australian relatives, have learned to move their legs independently of each other for climbing,

The Americas

The herds of wild horses now roaming the western deserts of the USA are descendents of domesticated animals that escaped and turned feral. It is widely thought that the horse was introduced into northern America by the Spanish, in the 16th century. In fact, horses and asses probably first evolved there. The asses died out some 12,000 years ago, and the native horses became extinct about 5,000 years later. This is one reason why the early escapee horses were so successful: they were not really an alien species, but were refilling an ecological niche that they had temporarily left vacant.

The reintroduction of the horse revolutionized the hunting techniques of the Plains Native Americans. Suddenly it became much easier to kill large numbers of the bison that were their main prey – a favourite tactic was to herd them over the edge of a cliff. Yet the Native Americans never killed more than they needed, and never wasted what they killed. The meat was preserved and the hides made tents, boats or clothing. Vertebral columns were covered with hide to serve as toboggan skids in winter, and shoulder-blades were turned into hoes. Even the animals' tendons found a use, as bow-strings or the webbing of snowshoes. At the dawn of the 19th century, there were up to 20 million bison on the American prairies. Early European settlers hunted these animals for their hides and for meat. Then, by the 1870s the bison were being killed solely for their tongues, which were considered a delicacy in Europe. Eventually they were slaughtered simply because it was easy, and provided a form of competitive sport. Their carcasses were left to rot on the prairie. By 1895, there were only 800 bison left. Captive breeding and the creation of game reserves allowed the numbers of bison living on the prairie to recover to more than 100,000 by 1992.

In the early days of the 19th century, a single herd of migrating bison might be so large that it would take five days to pass by. The bison, sweeping over the land, were sometimes known as "black fire". When they passed, they left the prairie grasses stripped down to the topsoil, which served the ecologically useful function of allowing herbs and shrubs to grow.

North and south

The extent of animal extermination in North America is illustrated even more clearly among its birds. In 1813, the backwoods naturalist Audubon described a gathering of flocks of blue-and-violet passenger pigeons in the prairies bordering Ohio: "The air was literally filled with pigeons. : the light of noon-day was obscured as by an eclipse; the dung fell in spots, not unlike melting flakes of snow; and the continued buzz of wings had a tendency to lull my senses to repose." He calculated that 11 hundred million pigeons flocked to the area in just three days. Their numbers were so great that: "The pigeons, arriving by thousands, alighted everywhere, one above another, until solid masses the size of hogsheads were formed on the branches all around. Here and there the perches gave way with a crash, and, falling to the ground, destroyed hundreds of birds beneath." Audubon also described the massacre that took place, not just by gunfire, but by men who simply stood and waved poles back and forth in front of the oncoming tide of birds. In 1914, the last surviving passenger pigeon died in Cincinatti zoo.

Hummingbirds have fostered as many misconceptions as any other animal. They are considered native to South America and the tropics, but this is only because they have been wiped out in the north. The first description of a living hummingbird comes from northeastern America, and hummingbirds were once common from Alaska to Cape Horn. When they were first discovered, they were thought to be "plumed butterflies", the next stage in the insects' metamorphosis after caterpillar, pupa and imago. They are still widely reported as feeding only on nectar, whereas their staple diet is actually small insects. The nectar simply provides them with enough energy for the rapid wingbeats that allow them to hover, and whose noise gives them their name.

Amazonia

The Amazon River originates in the Andean Mountains scarcely 100 miles (160km) from the Pacific Ocean, and crosses the width of a continent to empty into the Atlantic. Its waters pour into the ocean with such force that the sea is diluted some 100 miles (160km) out from the river mouth, yet the effects of the tide can be measured 600 miles (1,000km) inland. Because of this vast transition zone between river and sea, many marine animals have evolved freshwater forms, among them relatives of the Old World manatees that inspired the tales of mermaids told by Horace and Ovid. Christopher Columbus was the first European to describe the New World manatee: "In a bay on the coast of Hispaniola I saw three sirens; but they were not nearly as beautiful as old Horace's." The discovery of the Amazonian manatee – which weeps when excited, and suckles its young with human-like, hemispherical breasts – only reinforced the mermaid legends. Pink Amazonian dolphins were another species to make the transition to fresh water, using their sonar – sounds projected through a focusing, fatty lens in the dolphin's head – to navigate in the murky river water.

Estuarine dolphins and fishermen have forged a partnership in southern Brazil, where the water is too dark for the humans to see the mullet they are trying to catch. When the dolphins locate a shoal with their sonar, they splash to inform the fishermen, and in return take their pick from the confused and panicking mullet fleeing the fishermens' nets. They have not been trained: the practice arose naturally several hundred years ago. Young dolphins learn the behaviour by watching their parents.

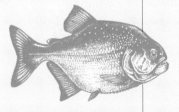

The ferocious reputation of the piranha fish is not entirely justified. Amazonian Indians frequently swim in the presence of piranha shoals, and there is even a species of piranha that eats only fruit. However, the merest scent of blood sends the flesh-eating varieties into a frenzy, and with their razor-sharp, diamond-shaped teeth they can strip a cow or a capybara to the bone in minutes.

Animal Distribution

Climatic variations, oceans, mountain chains and deserts all form physical barriers that can act to stop animal populations from increasing their range. Often these barriers will have developed after the evolution of a species, isolating it in a number of far-flung communities that can seem as if they were never connected. For example, there are two distinct wild gorilla populations, separated by the geologically recent giant loop of the River Zaire. But the greatest influence on the spread of animals has been the movements, separations and rejoinings of the continents since complex living organisms first started colonizing the land more than 400 million years ago (at which time South America, Africa, Antarctica, Australia and India formed one major land mass, called Gondwana, North America and northern Europe a second, called Euramerica, and Siberia the third). Continental migration has meant that the world can be divided into six "zoogeographic regions", with more than half the existing families of mammals restricted to one or other of them. Many of the remaining families exist in only two or three of the regions, and only eleven families have a truly worldwide distribution: the shrews; the squirrels and chipmunks; the hamsters and voles; the rabbits and hares; the deer; the bears; the dogs; the cats; the weasels and badgers; the cattle, sheep and antelope; and the rats and mice.

The human influence on animal distribution can be gauged by how many representatives of these worldwide families have been domesticated, and transported around the planet by their owners. The rats and mice were distributed unwittingly by the same people. Domestic animals are easier to tend in open ground, and the pollen record shows a marked increase in deforestation with the coming of agriculture, with all that this implies for forest-dwelling species. However, even in pre-agricultural times it seems that the Mesolithic peoples of northern Europe had used stone tools and fire to clear areas of forest, because open glades increased the numbers of red deer on which they depended.

No one is sure why 55 of the largest mammals of North America became extinct more or less simultaneously, around 11,000 years ago. It was long thought that the crucial factor was climatic change, but in 1967 the anthropologist Peter Martin pointed out that similar extinctions occurred at different times in other parts of the world, and coincided with the arrival of weapon-using humans. Most of the creatures that disappeared were large herbivores – such as the giant ground sloth – and flightless birds: precisely the cumbersome, meat-rich creatures that hunters would have preferred. These may be the first extinctions ever caused by humans.

The regions where species of animals and plants were first domesticated or cultivated, probably the first of them being wheat, more than 10,000 years ago. Although archaeological evidence suggests that some creatures – such as dogs, which would have been useful hunting companions – were tamed long before the first crops were planted, most of the animals that were captured and domesticated were initially pests, lured to human settlements by this new, concentrated, easily accessible food source.

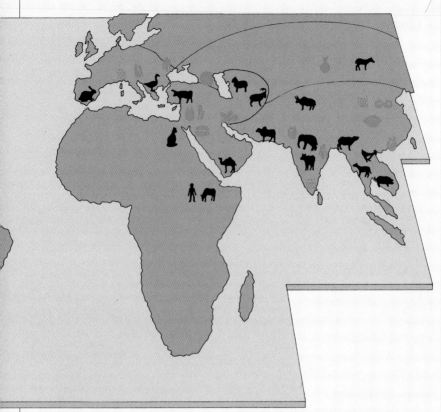

Central and South America

 Maize

Red pepper

Llama

Peanut

Pineapple

Potato

Runner bean

Tomato

Europe

Goose

Millet

Oats

Rabbit

Rye

Middle East and Africa

Alfalfa

Aurochs cattle

Barley

Camel

Goat

Lentil

Sheep

Wheat

Cat

Ass

Human

Central Asia

Apple

Horse

Onion

Yak

Southeast Asia, India, China

Bibos cattle

Dog

Elephant

Fowl

Lemon

Millet

Rice

Pig

Soya bean

Sugar cane

Water buffalo

Zebus cattle

Glossary

Anthropomorphism attributing human form or motivations to non-human beings or inanimate objects.

Australopithecus literally "southern ape". Regarded as the first hominid, and as such the first upright predecessor of the human being, *Homo sapiens sapiens*. Recently discovered fragments of skull and teeth of *Australopithecus ramidus* in Ethiopia may provide the "missing link" at the evolutionary divergence of humans from apes.

Avatar embodiment of a (strictly Hindu) god or principle. Vishnu appeared on Earth in ten different avatars.

Babylonia a culture that arose between the Tigris and Euphrates rivers (modern southern Iraq) *c.*4000BC.

Bestiary an illustrated book on animals, real and mythical, written in the Middle Ages. The stories point to a moral, often Christian, and have had an enduring effect on European folklore.

Classical antiquity the ancient Greek or Roman civilizations.

Classification the organization of animals in a hierarchy of groupings. Species are the basic unit of classification. A species is a type of organism distinguishable from all other types. Members of a species can breed with each other, but different species are not usually able to interbreed. The tiger is a distinct species. (Within a species there are subspecies, which clearly have some differences from each other, but are nevertheless able to breed with each other. The Siberian tiger and the Bengal tiger are both subspecies. Breeds are a type of subspecies created by humans, through the selective mating of the members of a species.) A genus is a group of related species: the tiger belongs to the genus *Panthera*, or big cats. A family contains related genera: the big cats belong to the family *Felidae*, or cats. An order contains related families: the cats belong to the order *Carnivora*, the carnivores. A class contains related orders: the carnivores belong to the class *Mammalia*, the mammals. A phylum, or sometimes sub-phylum, contains related classes: the mammals belong to the sub-phylum *Vertebrata*, the animals with backbones. The *Vertebrata* belong to the phylum *Chordata*, the creatures, such as sea squirts, that at some stage have a dorsal supporting rod. A kingdom contains related phyla: the *Chordata* belong to the kingdom *Animalia*, the multi-celled animals. (What is popularly called "the Animal Kingdom" technically contains three kingdoms: the *Animalia*; the *Monera*, or single-celled animals without a nucleus, such as bacteria; and the *Protista*, or single-celled animals with a nucleus.)

Collective unconscious a term used by Carl Gustav Jung to describe a deeply buried level of the human psyche which contains universal symbols and images gathered from our remote past.

Confucianism a philosophy and religion founded by Confucius in the 6th century BC. As much a code of conduct as a system of metaphysics.

Cosmic egg the origin of the world in many cultures, from Fijian to Finnish.

Cosmic tree see World tree.

Cosmogony pertaining to the birth of the universe; cosmogonic myths relate how the universe was created.

Culture hero a heroic, generally legendary, figure who performs extraordinary feats in the course of laying the foundations of a society.

Dharma conforming to religious law, custom, duty, or one's own quality or character, thereby accepting one's place in the universe. In Hinduism and Buddhism, correct practice of dharma leads to spiritual advancement.

DNA deoxyribonucleic acid, an organic molecule that constitutes genes.

Dreamtime the time of the creation of the world, according to Australian Aboriginals. A spiritual rather than a chronological era.

Ego the term used by Sigmund Freud to denote that portion of the personality experienced as the "Self", which is in contact with the world through the avenues of perception.

Evolution the genetic changes that occur in successive generations of a population of organisms, often resulting in the increased adaptation of the population to its environment.

Family see Classification.

Fertile Crescent a roughly crescent-shaped area of fertile land stretching from the Persian Gulf to the Nile Valley, where the ancient civilizations of the Middle East and the Mediterranean began.

Four Sacred Creatures, also known as the Four Auspicious Creatures in Chinese mythology, the tortoise, phoenix, dragon and unicorn, which were animals of good omen.

Gene the hereditary unit of an organism, which controls its physical characteristics.

Genus see Classification.

Heraldry the art or science of armorial bearings. Originally painted on banners and shields to differentiate factions in battle. Heraldic animals are used in coats of arms to symbolize the chivalrous qualities of an individual or family.

Hittites an Indo-European people who appeared in the region that corresponds to modern Turkey near the beginning of the second millennium BC, and by *c*.1350BC had become a dominant Middle Eastern power. Their empire lasted less than 300 years.

Hominid abbreviation of *Hominidae*, the mammalian family to which humans belong genetically.

Id the term used by Sigmund Freud to denote the primal pleasure-seeking passions of humans. He regarded the id as characterized by base instincts, antisocial and illogical. It is modified by the ego and the superego.

Jainism an Indian philosophy and religion founded in the 6th century BC which has no creator god, a doctrine of reincarnation and a central ethic of causing harm to no living thing.

Native American term referring to the indigenous inhabitants of North America.

Neanderthals cave dwellers who used stone tools, made fires and buried their dead. They probably arose between glacial periods, more than 100,000 years ago, and are thought to have died out, or been exterminated by more modern humans, some 35,000 years ago. At first Neanderthals were classified as a separate species (*Homo neanderthalensis*), but more recently they have been regarded as a subspecies of *Homo sapiens*.

Paleolithic literally "Old Stone Age". In human development, the period characterized by the use of rudimentary chipped stone tools, from 2.5 million years ago until the beginning of the Mesolithic period ("Middle Stone Age"), *c*.8500BC.

Primate the highest order of mammals, which includes humans, apes and monkeys. Defining characteristics include the possession of a collarbone, a unique fissure pattern on the cerebral cortex of the brain, and the ability to oppose thumb and fingers.

Psychopomp a guide who conducts spirits or souls to the other world.

Shaman a ritual specialist, an important figure in traditional societies in Asia, the Americas and parts of Africa, who contacts the spirits and communes with them in order to cure, divine or send magical illness. Often confused with witchdoctors, medicine men or sorcerers.

Shape-shifting the ability of supernatural and gifted beings to take on the form of an animal or some natural phenomenon, such as a storm.

Species see Classification.

Spirit-animal the spiritual essence of an animal, sometimes benevolent, often a danger to humankind which must be placated or otherwise dealt with. Spirit-animals may be all-knowing and can be forced to impart knowledge by a powerful human medium.

Superego a term used by Sigmund Freud to describe that part of our psychic apparatus concerned with social ideals and the rules and restrictions imposed by society on human behaviour; the conscience.

Taoism a religious and philosophical system that probably developed in China some time in the 4th century BC. It emphasizes spontaneity, simplicity and mystical experience, which is the only way to experience the Tao, the Absolute creative energy and beginning and end of all things.

Three Senseless Creatures in Chinese Buddhism, the deer represents love-sickness, the tiger anger and the monkey greed.

Totem a sacred animal, plant or object with a peculiar kinship to an individual or a society. Common in Native North and South American, Australian Aboriginal and Pacific Island cultures.

Traditional society a culture operating according to its own system of beliefs and practices, and generally uninfluenced by global civilizations or the advances of science.

Trickster a term applied to ambiguous supernatural figures which may be creative or subversive. Often mischievously cunning, they embody the principle of chaos and disorder but are also culture-bringers. Sometimes they take human form, but they are usually conceived as animals such as the raven and fox.

Yin and yang in Chinese philosophy and religion, the female-male principle, symbolizing the balanced complementariness of opposites. The yin represents the dark, female, generative processes, while the yang is the light, male and active principle.

World tree the tree represents the universe with its roots in the underworld, the trunk on earth and the branches growing up into the heavens. An important symbol in many mythologies, for example Norse.

Bibliography

Bostock, S. St. C. *Zoos and Animal Rights* Routledge, London, 1993

Campbell, J. *The Masks of God* Arkana/Penguin, Harmondsworth, 1987

Campbell, J. *The Way of the Animal Powers* Summerfield Press, London, 1983/Alfred van der Marck Editions, New York, 1983

Catlin, G. *North American Indians* Dover Publications, New York, 1973

Clutton-Brock, J. *Horse Power* Natural History Museum Publications, London, 1992

Clutton-Brock, J. (ed.) *The Walking Larder: Patterns of Domestication, Pastoralism, and Predation* Unwin Hyman, London, 1989

Cohen, D. *The Encyclopaedia of Monsters* Michael O'Mara Books, London, 1982

Cooper, J. C. *Symbolic & Mythological Animals* The Aquarian Press, London, 1992

Cooper, J. C. *An Illustrated Encyclopaedia of Traditional Symbols* Thames & Hudson, London, 1993

Cordry, D. *Mexican Masks* University of Texas Press, Austin, 1980

Cotterell, A. *A Dictionary of World Mythology* Oxford University Press, Oxford, 1990

Cox, C. B. and Moore, P. D. *Biogeography: An Ecological and Evolutionary Approach* Blackwell Scientific Publications, London, 1973

Crook, J. H. *Social Behaviour in Birds and Mammals* Academic Press, London, 1970

Crane, E. *The Archaeology of Beekeeping* Duckworth, London, 1983

Darnton, R. *The Great Cat Massacre* Vintage Books, 1985

Darwin, C. *On the Origin of Species* John Murray, London, 1859

Darwin, C. *The Descent of Man* John Murray, London, 1871

Dewey, D. *Bears* Headline Book Publishing, London, 1991

Downer, J. *Supersense: Perception in the Animal World* BBC Books, London, 1988

Downer, J. *Lifesense* BBC Books, London, 1991

Driver, H. E. *The Indians of North America* University of Chicago Press, Chicago, 1969

Edmunds, M. *Defence in Animals* Longman, London, 1974

Eliade, M. *Shamanism: Archaic Techniques of Ecstasy* Princeton University Press, Princeton, 1974

Fiedler, L. *Freaks: Myths and Images of the Secret Self* Simon and Schuster, New York, 1978

Penguin Books, London, 1981

Fontana, D. *The Secret Language of Symbols* Pavilion, London, 1993/Chronicle, San Francisco, 1993

Fox, M. W. *Abnormal Behavior in Animals* Saunders, Philadelphia, 1968

Frazer, J. G. *The Golden Bough* Macmillan, London, 1990

Furst, P. T. *Hallucinogens and Culture* Chandler & Sharp, San Fransisco, 1976

George, W. and Yapp, B. *The Naming of the Beasts* Duckworth, London, 1991

Gordon, S. *The Encyclopedia of Myths and Legends* Headline Book Publishing, London, 1992

Gould, S. J. *The Wonderful Life* Penguin, Harmondsworth, 1989

Graves, R. *The Greek Myths* Penguin, Harmondsworth, 1960

Griffin, D. R. *Animal Thinking* Harvard University Press, Cambridge, Mass., 1984

Hare, T. (ed.) *Nature Worlds* Pan Macmillan/ Duncan Baird Publishers, London, 1994/published in the USA as *Habitats* Macmillan Inc., New York, 1994

Huevelmans, B. *On the Track of Unknown Animals* Rupert Hart Davies, London, 1962

Hinnells, J. R. *Dictionary of Religions* Penguin, Harmondsworth, 1984

Hulme, F. E. *Natural History Lore and Legend* Quaritch, London 1895

Ingold, T. (ed.) *What is an Animal?* Unwin Hyman, London, 1988

Klein, R. G. *The Human Career* University of Chicago Press, Chicago, 1989

Larousse Encyclopedia of Mythology Paul Hamlyn, London, 1960

Lehner, E. and J. *A Fantastic Bestiary: Beasts and Monsters in Myth and Folklore* Tudor, New York, 1969

Ley, W. *The Lungfish, the Dodo and the Unicorn* Viking Press, New York, 1952

Lopez, B. H. *Of Wolves and Men* Dent, London 1978

Lorenz, K. *Studies in Animal and Human Behaviour* Harvard University Press, Cambridge, Mass., 1971

Loxton, H. *The Noble Cat* Merehurst Fairfax, London, 1990

Macdonald, D. (ed.) *The Encyclopedia of Mammals Vols. 1 and 2* George Allen & Unwin, London, 1984

Mader, S. *Biology* Wm. C. Brown Publishers, New York and London, 1990

Manning, A. and Serpell, J. (eds.) *Animals and Society* Routledge, London, 1993

Midgley, M. *Beast and Man: the roots of human nature* Harvester Press, 1981

Miller, M. and Taube, K. *The Gods and Symbols of Ancient Mexico and the Maya* Thames & Hudson, London, 1993

Moore, J. H. *The Universal Kinship* Centaur Press, London, 1992

Morphy, H. *Animals into Art* Unwin Hyman, London, 1989

Morris, D. *Animalwatching: A Field Guide to Animal Behaviour* Jonathan Cape, London, 1990

Morris, D. *The Naked Ape* Jonathan Cape, London, 1967

Mundkur, B. *The Cult of the Serpent* State University of New York Press, New York, 1983

Penny, M. *Alligators and Crocodiles* Boxtree, London, 1991

Pliny the Elder (trans. by J. F. Healy) *Natural History: a selection* Penguin, Harmondsworth, 1991

Polo, M. (trans. by A. Ricci) *The Travels of Marco Polo* Routledge and Kegan Paul, London, 1931

Ray, D. J. *Eskimo Art* University of Washington Press, Seattle, 1977

Reader's Digest *The Living World of Animals* Reader's Digest, London, 1970

Reader's Digest *Sharks: silent hunters of the deep* Reader's Digest, London, 1990

Reichel-Dolmatoff, G. *Amazonian Cosmos* University of Chicago Press, Chicago, 1971

Reynolds, V. *The Apes* Cassell, London, 1968

Rheingold, H.L. *Maternal Behavior in Mammals* Wiley, New York, 1963

Ricciuti, E. R. *Killer Animals* Walker, New York, 1976

Ritvo, H. *The Animal Estate* Penguin, Harmondsworth, 1990

Saunders, N. J. *People of the Jaguar* Souvenir Press, London, 1989

Saunders, N. J. *The Cult of the Cat* Thames & Hudson, London, 1991

Serpell, J. A. *In the Company of Animals* Blackwell, Oxford, 1986

Thomas, K. *Man and the Natural World* Penguin, Harmondsworth, 1983

Toynbee, J. M. C. *Animals in Roman Life and Art* Thames & Hudson, London, 1978

Tresidder, J. *The Hutchinson Dictionary of Symbols* Helicon, Oxford/Duncan Baird Publishers, London, 1995

Ucko, P. and Rosenfeld, A. *Palaeolithic Cave Art* McGraw-Hill, London and New York, 1967

Urton, G. (ed.) *Animal Myths and Metaphors in South America* University of Utah Press, Salt Lake City, 1985

Van Lawick-Goodall, J. *In the Shadow of Man* McGraw-Hill, London and New York, 1969

Vitebsky, P. *The Shaman* Macmillan/Duncan Baird Publishers, London 1995/Little, Brown & Company, New York, 1995

Williams, H. *Whale Nation* Jonathan Cape, London, 1988

Williams, H. *Sacred Elephant* Jonathan Cape, London, 1989

Willis, R. (ed.) *Signifying Animals: human meaning in the natural world* Unwin Hyman, London, 1990

Willis, R. *World Mythology: the illustrated guide* Simon & Schuster, London, 1993/Holt, New York, 1993

Woodward, I. *The Werewolf Delusion* Paddington Press, New York and London, 1979

Index

Picture Credits

The publisher thanks the photographers and organisations for their kind permission to reproduce the following photographs in this book:

Abbreviations
B below; **C** centre; **T** top; **L** left; **R** right
DBP Duncan Baird Publishers
MEPL Mary Evans Picture Library
NHPA Natural History Photographic Agency
WFA Werner Forman Archive
MH Michael Holford
AA&A Ancient Art and Architecture

1 NHPA/Stephen Dalton; **2** Colorphoto Hans Hinz; **7** ET Archive/British Library; **8–9** ET Archive/British Museum; **10** Planet Earth Pictures/John Downer; **11** Survival Anglia/Dieter and Mary Plage; **12T** Hutchison Library/Robin Constable; **12B** Bruce Coleman/John Shaw; **13** Zefa; **14T** Bruce Coleman/Jens Rydell; **14B** Science Photo Library/Wil and Deni McIntyre; **15TL** NHPA/Stephen Dalton; **15TC** NHPA/Peter Johnson; **15TR** NHPA/ANT; **15B** NHPA/William Paton; **16T** Colorphoto Hans Hinz; **16B** Survival Anglia/Rick Price; **17** Fortean Picture Library; **18T** Peter Bently; **18B** Bodleian Library, Oxford; **19T** Science Photo Library; **19B** Skriften Von Carl von Linne volume 5 Iter Lapponicum 1732; **20T** Zefa; **20B** Robert Harding Picture Library/Christina Cascoigne; **21** Frank Spooner Pictures/C. H. Dumas; **22L** MEPL; **22R** © British Museum; **23T** Survival Anglia/Dieter and Mary Plage; **23B** Image Select/Ann Ronan; **24** The Bodleian Library, Oxford; **25L** Zefa; **25R** *Songs of Humpback Whales* by Roger S Payne & Scott Mcray; **26B** Felix Darley, © Kansas State Historical Society; **27A** N. J. Saunders ; **27B** Hutchison Library/Michael MacIntyre; **28** Zefa; **29T** Hutchison Library/Michael MacIntyre; **29B** Image Select/Ann Ronan; **30** Bridgeman Art Library/Gavin Graham Gallery, London; **30–31** Bridgeman Art Library/Giraudon; **31** Ann & Bury Peerless; **32** MEPL; **32–33** Colorsport; **33** MEPL; **34–35** Robert Harding Picture Library/Nick Bayntum; **36** MH/Victoria & Albert Museum; **37T** Images/Charles Walker Collection; **37BL** Sue Sharples/DBP; **37BR** MH/British Museum; **38** MH/British Museum; **39** WFA/Private Collection; **40** MH/British Museum; **41T** Biblioteque L'Assemblée National © Darbownicas; **41B** Copyright British Museum; **42** MH/British Museum; **43T** WFA; **43B** Scala,

Florence; **44L** NHPA/ANT; **44R** The Mansell Collection; **45T** Bruce Coleman/Erwin and Peggy Bauer; **45B** *1800 Woodcuts* by Thomas Bewick and his School, Dover Publications; **46–47** ET Archive; **47** Bridgeman Art Library/British Museum; **48** Bridgeman Art Library/Freud Museum; **49L** NHPA/Stephen Dalton; **49R** Images/Charles Walker Collection; **50** MH/British Museum; **51T** WFA/Musées Royaux du Cinquantenaire Brussels; **51B** AA&A/B Norman; **52–53** Images/Charles Walker Collection; **54T** Jean-Loup Charmet; **54BL** Hutchison Library; **54B** R. J. Kirschner/DBP; **55** Aspect Picture Library; **56T** *Heraldic Crests* by James Fairbairn, Dover Publications; **56B** MEPL; **57T** *Heraldic Crests* by James Fairbairn, Dover Publications; **57B** Weidenfeld & Nicholson; **58–59** National Museum, Copenhagen/Kit Weiss; **60** Jean-Loup Charmet; **61TL** The Kobal Collection; **61TR** Bruce Coleman/Peter Davy; **61B** WFA/Private Collection; **62T** AA&A; **62C** Zefa; **62B** WFA/C. E. Strouhal; **63T** Sonia Halliday Photographs/Laura Lushington; **63B** MH/Victoria & Albert Museum; **64** MH/Musée Cernuschi, Paris; **64–65** Zefa; **65T** MH/Victoria & Albert Museum; **65B** Bridgeman Art Library/Private Collection; **66** Frank Lane Picture Agency/Silvestris; **67T** American Museum of Natural History; **67C** Peter Gorman; **67B** AA&A; **68** Bridgeman Art Library/House of Masks, Delos, Greece; **69L** MH; **69R** Pitt Rivers Museum, Oxford; **70T** ET Archive/British Library; **70B** Adriano Bacchella; **71T** C. M. Dixon; **71TR** WFA/The Egyptian Museum, Cairo; **71B** AA&A; **72** WFA/Field Museum of Natural History, Chicago; **72–73** WFA/British Museum; **73T** Scala, Florence; **73B** Zefa; **74** WFA/C. E. Strouhal; **75TL** Zefa; **75TR** ET Archive/Tate Gallery; **75B** Bridgeman Art Library/Lauros-Giraudon; **76T** Images/Charles Walker Collection; **76B** Zefa; **77T** C. M. Dixon; **77B** MEPL; **78–79** Zefa; **79TL** WFA/Alaska Gallery of Eskimo Art; **79TR** Department of Indian Affairs, Canada; **79B** ET Archive; **80** MH/Victoria & Albert Museum; **81L** Jean-Loup Charmet; **81R** Bruce Coleman/M. P. Kahl; **82T** *1800 Woodcuts* by Thomas Bewick and his School, Dover Publications; **82B** Images/Charles Walker Collection; **83T** Fortean Picture Library; **83B** AA&A; **84** WFA/Denpasar Museum, Bali; **85T** Reunion des Musées Nationaux; **85BL** C. M. Dixon; **85BR** Sonia Halliday Photographs; **86** ET Archive; **87TL**

AA&A; **87TR** Hutchison Library/Christina
Dodwell; **87B** MEPL; **88** Bridgeman Art Library;
89C M. S. Garretson from *The American Bison* ©
New York Zoological Society 1938; **89T** C. M.
Dixon; **89B** Jean-Loup Charmet; **90T** Hutchison
Library/Sarah Errington; **90B** C. M. Dixon; **91T**
MH; **91B** Scala, Florence; **92–93** MH/British
Museum; **94T** Images/Charles Walker Collection;
94B WFA/C. E. Strouhal; **94–95** Bridgeman Art
Library/Mausoleo di Galla Placidia, Ravenna; **95**
Scala, Florence; **96** MH/British Museum; **97T**
MH/Victoria & Albert Museum; **97BL** Justin
Kerr; **97BR** Zefa; **98** Justin Kerr; **99TL** Zefa;
99TR MH/Victoria & Albert Museum; **99B** Zefa;
100L Axel Poignant Archive/Cranstone; **100R**
MEPL; **101TL** WFA/Museum fur Volkerkunde,
Berlin; **101TR** *Animals*, Dover Publications; **101B**
C. M. Dixon; **102T** *Animals*, Dover Publications;
102B Hutchison Library/Juliet Highet; **103**
AA&A; **104T** Scala, Florence; **104B** MEPL; **105T**
Bruce Coleman/Austin James Stevens; **105B** Axel
Poignant Archive/Australian Museum, Sydney;
106 Images/Charles Walker Collection; **107T**
Beautyway – A Navaho Ceremonial published by
Bollingen Foundation Inc, Pantheon Books, New
York; **107BL** Japan Archives; **107BR** WFA/Brian
McElney, Hong Kong; **108T** WFA/Field Museum
of Natural History, Chicago; **108B** Axel Poignant
Archive; **109T** Images/Charles Walker Collection;
109B Justin Kerr; **110T** *Animals*, Dover
Publications; **110B** MEPL; **111L** Bruce Coleman/
Kim Taylor; **111R** AA&A; **112–113** NHPA/
Stephen Dalton; **114T** *Animals*, Dover
Publications; **114B** Bodleian Library, Oxford;
115T Scala, Florence; **115B** Sonia Halliday
Photogaphs/Andre Held; **116T** *Animals*, Dover
Publications; **116B** Jean-Loup Charmet; **117** UBC
Museum of Anthropology, Vancouver; **118T**
Bruce Coleman/J. L. G. Grande; **118B** *Curious
Woodcuts of Fanciful and Real Beasts* by Konrad
Gesner, Dover Publications; **119L** MEPL; **119R**
Royal Scottish Museum, Edinburgh; **120T**
Traditional Stencil Designs From India by
Pradumna and Rosalba Tana, Dover Publications;
120B Scala, Florence; **121T** *Curious Woodcuts of
Fanciful and Real Beasts* by Konrad Gesner,
Dover Publications; **121BL** ET Archive; **121BR**
Andes Press Agency/Carolo Reyes; **122** ET
Archive/Egyptian Museum, Cairo; **123T** Scala,
Florence; **123B** Victoria & Albert Museum; **124T**
Sonia Halliday Photographs/Laura Lushington;
124B Bridgeman Art Library/San Marco, Venice;
125T Frank Lane Picture Agency/Eric and David
Hoskings; **125BL** Robert Estall Photographs;
125BR ET Archive; **126L** *Animals*, Dover
Publications; **126R** ET Archive/Bibli

oteca Estense Modena; **127T** Jean-Loup Charmet;
127B Zefa; **128L** WFA; **128R** AA&A; **129L** Zefa;
129R Sonia Halliday Photographs/Laura
Lushington; **130T** *Animals*, Dover Publications;
130B C. M. Dixon; **131T** Bruce Coleman/Frans
Lanting; **131B** WFA/Smithsonian Institution,
Washington; **132L** WFA/Field Museum of
Natural History, Chicago; **132R** Angelo Hornak;
133 The Image Bank/Paolo Curto; **134** Royal
Astronomical Society; **134–135** Frank Lane
Picture Agency/Michael Gore; **135T** MEPL; **135B**
© British Museum; **136** MH/Anne Breton, Paris;
137L Bridgeman Art Library/British Library;
137TR MH/Private Collection; **137BR** WFA/N. J.
Saunders; **138** Zefa; **138B** *Curious Woodcuts of
Fanciful and Real Beasts* by Konrad Gesner,
Dover Publications; **139** Musée de l'Homme,
Paris; **140** Scala, Florence; **140–141** *Curious
Woodcuts of Fanciful and Real Beasts* by Konrad
Gesner, Dover Publications; **141T** Scala, Florence;
141B Bruce Coleman/Jane Burton; **142–3** Images/
Charles Walker Collection; **144** Range/Bettman/
UPI; **145T** Jean-Loup Charmet; **145B** John Cleare
Mountain Camera; **146T** MH/British Museum;
146B Scala, Florence; **147T** Scala, Florence; **147B**
Tate Gallery Publications; **148–9** Royal Musées
des Beaux-Arts, Brussels; **149T** Scala, Florence;
149B MH; **150T** Fortean Picture Library; **150B**
Scala, Florence; **151T** *Curious Woodcuts of
Fanciful and Real Beasts* by Konrad Gesner,
Dover Publications; **151B** AA&A; **152T**
Bridgeman Art Library/Palazzo Sandi-Porto
(Cipollata), Venice; **152B** Bridgeman Art
Library/K & B News Foto, Florence; **153L**
MH/Victoria & Albert Museum; **153R** Fortean
Picture Library; **154B** Sonia Halliday
Photographs/Laura Lushington; **155T** WFA/State
Museum Berlin; **155B** MH/Victoria & Albert
Museum; **156** Bridgeman Art Library/Wallace
Collection, London; **156–157** *Curious Woodcuts of
Fanciful and Real Beasts* by Konrad Gesner,
Dover Publications; **157T** ET Archive; **157B**
Hulton Deutsch Collection/Kenneth Wilson;
158T Science Photo Library; **158B** Jean-Loup
Charmet; **159** Metropolitan Museum of Art/
Harris Brisbane Dick Fund 1942 (42.45.1); **160**
MH/Victoria & Albert Museum; **161** *Animals*,
Dover Publications; **162B** *Animals*, Dover
Publications; **162T** Frank Spooner Pictures/
Piquemal; **163** Barnaby's/Presseverlag; **164–8**
Animals, Dover Publications.

Every effort has been made to trace copyright
holders. However, if there are any omissions we
would be happy to insert them in future editions.